Building Up
One Another

Building Up
One Another

Gene Getz

David C Cook®

transforming lives together

BUILDING UP ONE ANOTHER
Published by David C. Cook
4050 Lee Vance View
Colorado Springs, CO 80918 U.S.A.

David C. Cook Distribution Canada
55 Woodslee Avenue, Paris, Ontario, Canada N3L 3E5

David C. Cook U.K., Kingsway Communications
Eastbourne, East Sussex BN23 6NT, England

David C. Cook and the graphic circle C logo
are registered trademarks of Cook Communications Ministries.

LCCN 97173388
ISBN 978-1-56476-517-8
eISBN 978-0-7814-0667-3

© 1976 Gene Getz
First Edition published by Victor Books © 1976 Gene Getz, ISBN 0-88207-744-9

Editors: Jane Vogel, Barb Williams; Craig Bubeck, Sr. Editor over revision
Design: Pamela Poll Graphic Design, pampoll@aol.com
Cover Design: Sarah Schultz
Cover Photo: © iStock

Printed in the United States of America
Second Edition 1997

37 38 39 40 41 42

082511

Contents

Looking Ahead

Please read this opening section carefully and prayerfully. If you do not, you'll miss a very important overview of Scripture that is absolutely essential in understanding and effectively applying the "one another" exhortations outlined in the chapters to follow. Furthermore, you'll miss a very challenging testimony from the author regarding the way this study has impacted his own life and ministry. Note too that this introduction offers suggestions for launching a small group study.

The Editors

Several years ago, I made a wonderful discovery. It happened when I was a full-time professor interacting with my students at Dallas Theological Seminary about God's plan for the church. Their questions were penetrating and challenging! What is a healthy church? What does God expect from all believers? What makes a church a dynamic witness in the world?

All of these questions motivated me to investigate more deeply what is recorded in the letters written to the various New Testament churches. As I pursued this journey through the New Testament epistles, one major concept kept jumping off the pages of Scripture. Again and again I noticed exhortations regarding what believers are to do *for one another*. Paul, particularly, used the Greek word *allelon* nearly forty times to instruct Christians regarding their mutual responsibilities to their fellow believers.

Recently, I took a fresh look at this concept in the New Testament letters. As always happens, I uncovered some new insights that I missed the first time around. I'm anxious to share these discoveries with you. But first, let me share what happened as a result of my first journey.

More than I realized, my initial discovery of these "one another" exhortations was destined to impact my life dramatically for years to come—and the lives of many others. First, it became a key in unlocking the process Paul described in his Letter to the Ephesians. This great first-century church planter made it crystal clear that the "body of Christ" will never become a growing and dynamic community reflecting Christ's love unless "each part does its work." God's plan is that "the whole body" is to be "joined and held together by every supporting ligament" (Eph. 4:16). Total body function is absolutely essential if a local church is to become all God intended it to be!

A CHURCH I NEVER PLANNED TO START

During my initial interaction with my students at the seminary, several of them challenged me to start a church and to apply these "one another" injunctions at the grassroots level. At first, I was hesitant. After all, I had been a professor for nearly twenty years. But, I took this challenge seriously and helped several families start the first Fellowship Bible Church in Dallas. I served as pastor. Attendance exploded and I knew rather quickly I'd have to make a vocational decision. After a lot of reflection and prayer, I decided to give up my full-time professorship and become a full-time church planting pastor.

Since starting the first Fellowship Bible Church in 1972, it has multiplied into over a dozen churches in the Dallas metroplex and several hundred throughout the United States and even into foreign countries—such as Fellowship Bible Church in Warsaw, Poland.

Currently, I pastor Fellowship Bible Church North in Plano, Texas—which we launched in 1981—a church that has become a rapidly growing megachurch. Then in 1997, we launched Fellowship Bible Church of McKinney, Texas—another great mission field in the far north Dallas metroplex.

During these years of church planting experience, I've discovered that no emphasis is more important than to teach Christians what the Bible says about these "one another" injunctions. When I began to emphasize these great biblical truths in my pulpit ministry, in our orientation classes, in our leadership training sessions, and in our small group ministry (which we call minichurches), I've never seen more "body function" and "personal participation" take place among Christians. Furthermore, I've never observed more spiritual growth. This should not be surprising since this is why the Holy Spirit inspired the New Testament writers to record these wonderful exhortations. Over the years, pastors have shared with me again and again—face-to-face and by letter—that using these "one another" passages for sermons and group Bible study has totally changed the dynamics of their churches.

NEW INSIGHTS

As I recently revisited these "one anothers" in Scripture, I noticed something I'd missed—which is a marvelous reality regarding Scripture. There's always more to learn—no matter how carefully we've read and studied the Word of God. In what was probably Paul's first letter—the Epistle to the Galatians, he contrasted "the acts of the sinful nature" with "the fruit of the Spirit." Paul wrote:

> For the sinful nature desires what is contrary to the Spirit, and the Spirit what is contrary to the sinful nature. They are in conflict with each other [*allelon*] (Gal. 5:17).

In this instance, Paul used the "one another" or "each other" concept to show the marked difference between people who follow the "sinful nature" in their relationships with "one another" and those who "live by the Spirit" and "keep in step with the Spirit" (5:25). Throughout this entire passage, Paul was speaking "relationally"— not just regarding personal attitudes and actions. This is why he used plural pronouns to describe the way that the "acts of the sinful nature" are manifested among non-Christians and conversely, the way the "fruit of the Spirit" is reflected in the lives of Christians as they relate to one another.

This introduces us to a very fascinating dichotomy regarding the way the "one anothers" are outlined in the New Testament. They can actually be grouped under "the acts of the sinful nature" and "the fruit of the Spirit." When they are, we can see immediately what Paul had in mind when he stated that these two manifestations conflict with one another (5:17).

"THE ACTS OF THE SINFUL NATURE"

The acts of the sinful nature are obvious: sexual immorality, impurity and debauchery; idolatry and witchcraft; hatred, discord, jealousy, fits of rage, selfish ambition, dissensions, factions and envy; drunkenness, orgies and the like (Gal. 5:19-21).

Following is a list of negative "one another" statements that appear in several New Testament letters. Generally, these statements appear as they are translated in the *New International Version*. However, they are at times paraphrased in this list to demonstrate consistency and clarity, but without changing the specific meaning in the original text. These statements are as follows:

lusting for one another (Rom. 1:27)
judging one another (Rom. 14:13)
depriving one another (1 Cor. 7:5)
biting one another (Gal. 5:15a)
devouring one another (Gal. 5:15b)
destroying one another (Gal. 5:15c)
provoking one another (Gal. 5:26a)
envying one another (Gal. 5:26b)
lying to one another (Col. 3:9)
hating one another (Titus 3:3)
slandering one another (James 4:11)
grumbling against one another (James 5:9)

"THE FRUIT OF THE SPIRIT"

But the fruit of the Spirit is love, joy, peace, patience, kindness, goodness, faithfulness, gentleness and self-control (Gal. 5:22).

The following statements are *positive* "one another" exhortations. Again, they are at times paraphrased to demonstrate consistency and clarity, but in each instance reflect what the New Testament authors meant. Notice how these exhortations reflect the fruit of the Spirit:

members of one another (Rom. 12:5)
being devoted to another (Rom. 12:10a)
honoring one another (Rom. 12:10b)
being of the same mind toward one another (Rom. 12:16; 15:5)
loving one another (Rom. 13:8; 1 Thes. 3:12; 4:9; 2 Thes. 1:3; Heb. 10:24; 1 Peter 1:22; 1 John 3:11, 23; 4:7, 11, 12; 2 John 5)
edifying one another (Rom. 14:19)
accepting one another (Rom. 15:7)
instructing one another (Rom. 15:14)
greeting one another (Rom. 16:16; 1 Cor. 16:20; 2 Cor. 13:12; 1 Thes. 5:26; 1 Peter 5:14)
waiting for one another (1 Cor. 11:33)
caring for one another (1 Cor. 12:25)
serving one another (Gal. 5:13)
carrying one another's burdens (Gal. 6:2)
bearing with one another (Eph. 4:2; Col. 3:13)
being kind to one another (Eph. 4:32)
submitting to one another (Eph. 5:21; 1 Peter 5:5)
esteeming one another (Phil. 2:3)
encouraging one another (1 Thes. 4:18; 5:11, 14)
confessing sins to one another (James 5:16a)
praying for one another (James 5:16b)
offering hospitality to one another (1 Peter 4:9)
fellowshiping with one another (1 John 1:7)

One thing is very clear from these two lists of biblical statements. A church that is manifesting "the fruit of the Spirit" is practicing the "one another" injunctions that build up the body of Christ and lead to one-mindedness and unity. A church that is reflecting the "acts of the sinful nature" is carnal and is practicing the "one anothers" that keep the church worldly and in a state of disunity. Drawing on a New Testament example, this kind of church can be called a "Corinthian church" (1 Cor. 3:1-4). To quote Paul, the believers in Corinth were acting more like non-Christians than Christians. This is what Paul meant when he asked the question—"Are you not acting like mere men?" (1 Cor. 3:3).

OUR PERSONAL RESPONSIBILITY

How can your church—and mine—become a mature body of believers, reflecting "the fruit of the Spirit"? The answer is clear in Scripture. All believers must "live by the Spirit" and "keep in step with the Spirit" (Gal. 5:25). To do this, we must practice the "one another" exhortations that *build up* the body of Christ (Eph. 4:16) rather than destroying and dismantling it (Gal. 5:15). We must obey God's Word. In no instance are these exhortations qualified, such as "if you feel like it," "if it's convenient," "if it fits your personality," etc. These exhortations form a profile for *doing* the will of God! *All* Christians are to be involved. We must be committed to looking for opportunities to carry out these positive "one another" injunctions in our personal lives. At the same time we must avoid practicing the *negative* "one anothers." This is the essence of love!

EMPOWERED BY THE HOLY SPIRIT

It's true that all believers have a responsibility to practice the positive "one anothers" outlined in Scripture. If we love Jesus Christ and "one another," we will obey the Word of God (John 15:10; 1 John 5:3). However, this is far more than a human process that is based on an act of the will. It's a divine function where believers draw on the supernatural power of God.

First of all, Jesus prayed for all of us—which certainly includes our ability to *love one another as He loved us* (John 13:34). Jesus followed this "one another" command with that great prayer in John 17, which includes the following request:

> My prayer is not for them alone [the apostles]. I pray also for those who will believe in me through their message [believers of all time], that all of them may be one, Father, just as you are in me and I am in you. May they also be in us so that the world may believe that you have sent me (John 17:20-21).

Paul also made this supernatural process clear in his prayer for the Ephesian Christians—a prayer that is just as relevant for your church and mine. Note again that this prayer is for the total body—not just for individual members of the body. Again Paul used plural pronouns to make this point:

> I pray that out of his glorious riches he may strengthen you with power through his Spirit in your inner being, so that Christ may dwell in your hearts through faith. And I pray that you, being rooted and established in love, may have power, together with all the saints [believers of all time], to grasp how wide and long and high and deep is the love of Christ, and to know this love that surpasses knowledge—that you may be filled to the measure of all the fullness of God (Eph. 3:16-19).

The goal of Paul's prayer was that these believers might *"be filled to the measure of . . . the fullness of God"* (3:19). This is a succinct statement that summarizes the "fruit of the Spirit"—reflections of God's character—which is "love, joy, peace, patience, kindness, goodness, faithfulness, gentleness and self-control" (Gal. 5:22).

Paul culminated this prayer with a grand doxology—powerful verses that we have inscribed on huge banners that are displayed in the front of our own church. These verses remind all of us at least once a week that we can practice the positive "one anothers" with God's divine help:

Now to him who is able to do immeasurably more than all we ask or imagine, according to his power that is at work within us, to him be glory in the church and in Christ Jesus throughout all generations, for ever and ever! Amen (Eph. 3:20-21).

Against the backdrop of Paul's prayer in Ephesians 3, and his emphasis on the functioning body in chapter 4, we can now understand more fully what he meant in chapter 5 when he encouraged these believers to be "filled with the Spirit." Note once again that this is a corporate concept, directed at the entire church in Ephesus:

Do not get drunk on wine, which leads to debauchery. Instead, [as a body of believers] be filled with the Spirit. Speak to *one another*[1] with psalms, hymns and spiritual songs. Sing and make music in your heart to the Lord, always giving thanks to God the Father for everything, in the name of our Lord Jesus Christ (Eph. 5:18-20).

My personal prayer for you is that this study will impact your life and the life of your church as it has impacted me personally and the people I've had the privilege of ministering to over the years. If you take God's Word seriously and rely on the Holy Spirit to empower you, I'm confident it will!

SUGGESTIONS FOR GROUP LEADERS

Before you use this book in a small group setting, I would suggest you do several things:

1. Use a handout or overhead transparency to illustrate how the "one another" exhortations in the New Testament can be grouped under what Paul called "the

---

[1] The Greek word translated "one another" in this exhortation is *heautou*. When it is, it has the same basic meaning as *allelon*. (See also Eph. 4:32; Col. 3:13, 16; Heb. 3:13; 1 Peter 4:8.)

acts of the sinful nature" and the "fruit of the Spirit" (Gal. 5:19-22). Illustrate how these two categories of "one anothers" are in "conflict with each other."

2. Show how the "one another" exhortations selected for in-depth study in this book are foundational. For example, the first seven chapters of this book follow the "one anothers" as outlined by Paul in Romans 12–16—a section of this letter that clearly specifies how Christians are to live in view of God's mercy and grace that has been described in Romans chapters 1–11. This is significant since this letter is the most comprehensive and generic letter Paul ever wrote. In essence, Romans includes every-thing a church really needs to know to become mature. Following are the seven "one anothers" which appear sequentially in this letter:

   We are to be "members one of another" (Rom. 12:5, NASB).

   We are to be "devoted to one another" (Rom. 12:10a).

   We are to "honor one another" (Rom. 12:10b).

   We are to "be of the same mind with one another" (Rom. 15:5, NASB).

   We are to "accept one another" (Rom. 15:7).

   We are to "admonish one another" (Rom. 15:14, NASB).

   We are to "greet one another" (Rom. 16:16).

3. Spend some time in prayer asking the Holy Spirit to enlighten each participant to understand these exhorta-tions and to empower each one to practice them—begin-ning in this group process.

4. Conclude the session by reflecting on Paul's wonderful doxology in Ephesians 3:20-21.

—*Dr. Gene A. Getz*
Senior Pastor
Fellowship Bible Church North
Plano, Texas

Chapter One

Members of One Another

So we, who are many, are one body in Christ, and individually members one of another.

Romans 12:5, NASB

On one occasion, I distinctly remember watching an NFL football game. The Miami Dolphins were playing the Dallas Cowboys. The battle raged as each team attempted to put points on the scoreboard. The Cowboys took an early and commanding lead and maintained that lead most of the game.

But suddenly something happened to the Miami offense. Under the leadership of Dan Marino, the Dolphins' all-pro quarterback, the team suddenly began to move the ball. Like a precision machine that blended brilliance with intense emotion, they marched down the field and scored a touchdown. The display of unity was awesome! Every player did his part. No one missed an assignment.

I'm not a "football prophet" or even the "son" of one, but I remember suddenly predicting the outcome of that game. There was something you could sense and feel. The Dolphins seemed unstoppable—and they were. As I remember, they scored three touchdowns in the last few minutes and won the game.

There's power in unity—even in the purely human process of

athletics. Imagine what happens when this kind of effort is empowered and energized by the Holy Spirit. Actually, this is what Jesus had in mind when He prayed that the members of His body would be one as He was one with the Father (John 17:20-23)! This is a very important factor in not only building up the body of Christ in love but in being a dynamic witness in the world. This kind of unity defeats Satan! He is powerless to stop a church that is marching forward, "speaking the truth in love" (Eph. 4:15) and at the same time, demonstrating oneness "in heart and mind" (Acts 4:32).

DYNAMIC METAPHORS

The Apostle Paul used several metaphors to describe the church. In his Letter to the Corinthians, he used an *agricultural* analogy when he wrote—"You are God's *field*" (1 Cor. 3:5-9a). This metaphor beautifully correlates with Jesus' Parable of the Sower (Matt. 13:1-23; Mark 4:1-20; Luke 8:4-15).

In the same context, Paul used an *architectural* metaphor. He identified the Corinthians as "God's *building*" (1 Cor. 3:9). Paul went on to say that he had "laid a foundation . . . which is Jesus Christ," and other spiritual leaders built on this foundation (3:10-11).

Paul then used an *anatomical* metaphor—one of his most graphic illustrations for the church and one that is exclusively his own in the New Testament. Paul identified God's people as the "body of Christ." In his letters to the Romans, the Corinthians, the Ephesians, and the Colossians, he penned the word "*soma*"—which is translated "body"—more than thirty times to illustrate the functioning church. Approximately half of these times, he used the word to refer to the human, physical body with its many parts and members. In the other half, he applied the term to the church—the *body* of Christ.

THE "BODY" ANALOGY

Paul's most extensive use of the analogy of the human body appears in his Letter to the Corinthians, no doubt because of their carnality and immaturity and especially because of the disunity and divisions that existed among them (1 Cor. 1:10; 3:1-4). Because of their infant mentality, he made a special effort to spell out clearly and carefully the similarity between the "human body" and "Christ's body"—the church. In two extensive paragraphs, he used the Greek word "soma" fourteen times to illustrate just how the human body actually functions. Paul didn't want them to miss his point! And since he had previously experienced their inability to grasp spiritual truth, and since they were still unable to handle "solid food" (1 Cor. 3:1-2), he decided to make his point so clear that even the most immature Christian could understand what he was illustrating. Thus he wrote:

> Now the body [the human body] is not made up of one part but of many. If the foot should say, "Because I am not a hand, I do not belong to the body," it would not for that reason cease to be a part of the body. And if the ear should say, "Because I am not an eye, I do not belong to the body," it would not for that reason cease to be a part of the body. If the whole body were an eye, where would the sense of hearing be? If the whole body were an ear, where would the sense of smell be? But in fact God has arranged the parts in the body, every one of them, just as he wanted them to be. If they were all one part, where would the body be? As it is, there are many parts, but one body.
>
> The eye cannot say to the hand, "I don't need you!" And the head cannot say to the feet, "I don't need you!" On the contrary, those parts of the body that seem to be weaker are indispensable, and the parts that we think are less honorable we treat with special honor. And the parts that are unpresentable are treated with special modesty, while our presentable parts need no special treatment. But God has combined the members of the body and has given greater honor to the parts that lacked it, so that there should be no division in the body, but that its parts should have equal concern for each other. If one part suffers, every part suffers with it; if one part is honored, every part rejoices with it (1 Cor. 12:14-26).

There was no way that even the most immature Corinthian

Christian could miss Paul's message. His point of application was that Christians are "members one of another." Thus he concluded these lengthy, descriptive paragraphs by adding this concise statement and application: "Now *you* are the *body* of Christ, and *each one of you* is a part of it" (1 Cor. 12:27).

When Paul wrote to the Romans, he assumed that they understood the body metaphor—probably because these believers were a lot more mature than the Corinthians. Consequently, he simply stated the analogy and then immediately drove home his point of application:

The Metaphor

For just as we have many members in one body and all the members do not have the same function (Rom. 12:4, NASB).

The Application

So we, who are many, are one body in Christ, and individually members one of another (Rom. 12:5, NASB).

THREE IMPORTANT TRUTHS

In these passages, Paul emphasized three important principles that are just as relevant today as they were the day he wrote this letter.

1. Interdependence: No individual Christian can function effectively in isolation and alone.

One of my favorite sports is racquetball. I try to play regularly, remembering that "physical training is of some value" (1 Tim. 4:8a). However, I've discovered that if I'm going to compete at all in this sport, it's vitally important to develop coordination. Racquetball can be a ferociously fast game and adequate performance to compete is based on every part of the physical body "working together." This is particularly true of hand and eye coordination. But the game also demands the ability to anticipate what is about to happen and to be able to move into position even before your opponent returns the ball!

Just as "there are many parts of one body" in the makeup of

human beings that enable each of us to perform as individual physical units, so the body of Christ—the church—is made up of many
individual members. And each member is important. We are
indeed "members of one another." No member of Christ's body can
say, "I don't need you." We all need each other. If we are to win the
battle against our opponent in the spiritual realm, we must function as one dynamic unit. Interdependence and coordination are
absolutely essential.

2. Humility: No member of Christ's body should feel more important than any other member of Christ's body.

No Christian has exclusive rights to God's grace. This, perhaps, is one
of Paul's major teachings in the passages dealing with body function.
His emphasis is on humility! Though implied all the way through the
Corinthian passage (some Corinthians were saying, "I don't need
you" and "I'm more important than you"), Paul made it even clearer
in a parallel passage in his Roman letter:

> For by the grace given me I say to every one of you: Do not
> think of yourself more highly than you ought, but rather
> think of yourself with sober judgment, in accordance with the
> measure of faith God has given you (Rom. 12:3).

Paul's Ephesian letter reflects the same emphasis. Setting the
stage for discussing the purpose of gifts (as spelled out in Eph.
4:11-12), Paul wrote, "Be completely *humble* and *gentle*; be *patient*,
bearing with one another in love" (Eph. 4:2).

Why did Paul emphasize humility, gentleness, and patience in
this passage? Because, as he went on to say, "There is *one body* and
one Spirit" (Eph. 4:4). This is in essence the same thing he said to
the Corinthians: "For we were all baptized by *one Spirit into one
body*" (1 Cor. 12:13). In other words, no member of Christ's body
is more important than the other. Though one person may have a
more responsible position, in God's sight even the person who may
go unnoticed is just as important and necessary in the body of
Christ (1 Cor. 12:22-23).

Calvin Hill was one of the great NFL running backs of all time. However, he had one major area of vulnerability—his big toe! Though not the most appealing or attractive member of his huge frame, when he injured that big toe, he couldn't run effectively. To be able to do his job, he had to allow that member of his body to heal.

So it is in Christ's body, the church. Paul underscored this point in his Corinthian letter when he wrote:

> On the contrary, those parts of the body that seem to be weaker are indispensable, and the parts that we think are less honorable we treat with special honor. And the parts that are unpresentable are treated with special modesty
> (1 Cor. 12:22-23).

3. Unity: Every Christian should work hard at creating unity in the body of Christ.

This is why Paul immediately opened the Letter to the Corinthians by saying—"I appeal to you, brothers, in the name of our Lord Jesus Christ, that *all of you agree with one another* so that there may be no divisions among you and that you may be *perfectly united* in mind and thought" (1 Cor. 1:10). And this is why he also wrote to the Ephesians in the very same passage where he discussed body function: "*Make every effort* to keep the unity of the Spirit through the bond of peace" (Eph. 4:3). Emphasizing the same point, he wrote to the Romans—"Let us therefore *make every effort* to do what leads to peace and to *mutual edification*" (Rom. 14:19). Put another way, Paul was exhorting these Christians to do everything they could to "build up one another."

SPIRITUAL GIFTS

There are varied opinions among mature Christians regarding spiritual gifts—how many are in existence, how to recognize them, and how to use them. I'm convinced that the primary reason for this disagreement seems to be that we're misinterpreting these "gift pas-

sages." It may surprise you that these scriptural texts do not emphasize that we as *individuals* are to look for and to try to discover our
gifts so we can function as members of Christ's body.[1] Rather, we're
simply to use the gifts and abilities God has given us to build up the
body of Christ with a proper attitude. Paul assumed the presence of
these gifts and that these gifts were obvious to everyone.

A BIBLICAL EMPHASIS

Biblical writers emphasize two important truths. Again and
again we're told to become mature both corporately and personally. Corporate *maturity* is reflected in the degree of faith,
hope, and love—but especially love—that is developed in any
given local church. This is why Paul concluded 1 Corinthians
13 by saying: "And now these three remain: faith, hope and
love. But the greatest of these is love" (1 Cor. 13:13). This is
why he often introduced his letters to various churches by
thanking God for their faith, hope, and love. For example, he
wrote to the Thessalonians:

> We always thank God for all of you, mentioning you in our
> prayers. We continually remember before our God and Father
> your work produced by faith, your labor prompted by love,
> and your endurance inspired by hope in our Lord Jesus Christ
> (1 Thes. 1:2-3; see also 2 Thes. 1:3-4; Eph. 1:15-18; Col. 1:3-
> 5).

---

[1]Some Christians use 1 Corinthians 14:1 to teach that each Christian should
try to discover spiritual gifts. But a careful look at the text and context strong-
ly point to the fact that this is not what Paul was teaching. All the way through
this section of the Corinthian letter, Paul was directing his exhortations—not
to individuals—but to the corporate body of believers at Corinth. He specifically used the second person plural in the Greek language: "Eagerly [as a body]
desire spiritual gifts" (1 Cor. 14:1). In other words, Paul was telling the
Corinthians to desire that the greater gifts be manifested in their midst, not the
lesser gifts. It's clear that some Corinthian believers were giving primary attention to the lesser gifts rather than to apostleship, prophecy, and teaching,
which were the "greater gifts" (see 1 Cor. 12:28-31). This led to even more
prideful behavior and endless divisions and disagreements.

Personal maturity is reflected in the characteristics outlined by Paul in 1 Timothy chapter 3 and Titus chapter 1: being above reproach, morally pure, temperate, prudent, respectable, hospitable, able to teach,[2] not addicted to wine, not self-willed, not quick-tempered, not pugnacious, uncontentious, gentle, free from the love of money, a good manager of the home, respected by non-Christians, one who loves what is good, just, and devout (1 Tim. 3:1-13; Titus 1:5-9). Though these qualities are listed for those who become spiritual leaders, they are in reality a profile for Christian maturity that is detailed throughout the New Testament. Paul is simply saying that if anyone desires to be a spiritual leader, it's a wonderful goal. However, that person should make sure that he is a mature Christian. Paul then described what should characterize a mature believer.[3]

A PERSONAL EXPERIENCE

I've already shared some of my experiences in church planting, which have been very helpful in verifying what the Bible really teaches about the subject. Though it is dangerous to develop a "theological" position from our ministry activities, our experience should definitely help verify what the Bible teaches. The two should be in harmony.

One thing I've learned about spiritual gifts from both the study of Scripture and my church planting experience is never to get the "cart in front of the horse." Personally, I believe that to try to get believers to introspect and look for their gifts is doing just that. We're putting our emphasis in the wrong place. However, if we

---

[2] Some have interpreted "being able to teach," mentioned in 1 Timothy 3, as the gift of teaching. However, a careful look at the word translated "able to teach" in the original text, and Paul's use of it in 1 Timothy 3:2 and 2 Timothy 2:24, reveals that Paul was talking about a quality of life, not a particular pedagogical skill or a specific gift. Furthermore, it would be rather strange for Paul to single out the "gift of teaching" as a requirement for leadership and to omit the "gift of pastor" and the "gift of administration." This would be especially strange in view of the fact that Paul definitely instructed elders to be responsible for the teaching, shepherding, and managing responsibilities of a church.

[3] For an extensive and practical treatment of each of these qualities, see *The Measure of a Man* by Gene A. Getz, published by Regal Books.

teach believers how to become both corporately and personally mature in Christ, we'll see unusual spiritual growth in their lives. Furthermore, if we teach all believers how to practice the positive "one another exhortations" through obedience and reliance on the Holy Spirit, we'll see more body function take place than ever before. We'll avoid confusion and misunderstandings, and we'll see believers naturally and in a Spirit-directed way begin to use their gifts and talents maturely and humbly—to build up others rather than calling attention to themselves. To focus on our "gifts" is to focus on ourselves. To focus on maturity and building up the body of Christ is to focus on God and others.

A VERY IMPORTANT FIRST STEP

Once you understand what the Bible teaches about the "one another" concepts, take a close look at the structures of your church. Is it organized for "body function" to take place or is it organized for only certain high-profile people to participate?

When a church is small, it's easy to give opportunity for people to participate when the whole church meets corporately. However, as a church grows, it becomes more difficult. Consequently, forms and structures need to be developed to enable Christians to minister to one another. As Fellowship Churches, we've developed a small group ministry we've called "minichurches." These small groups normally meet in homes a couple of times a month and are led by lay pastors. They are designed to complement the larger meetings of the church when it meets for worship, celebration, and learning the Word of God. It's in these small groups that real body function takes place. Without this experience, we're out of harmony with what the Bible teaches about every part being necessary for the body of Christ to build itself up in love (Eph. 4:16).

Some churches use adult Sunday School classes to meet this need. Unfortunately, in some churches these classes simply become another "teaching-preaching" session with little, if any, "body function" taking place.

What is your church doing to make it possible for Christians to practice the "one another" exhortations? How are your forms and structures contributing to this process or hindering this process?

DISCUSSION GUIDE FOR SMALL GROUPS

OPENING

Spend some time getting acquainted with one another at the beginning of this first session. At the very least, be sure everyone knows everyone else's name.

Have each person complete these sentences:

If I could be any part of the human body, I would want to be

_____because_____

_____

_____.

The part of the body that I think I am most like is

_____because_____

_____

_____.

Together develop a list of group expectations or goals for your study of this book. Many small groups like to write a group "covenant" outlining what each member will do to support the

---

GROUP COVENANT

As members of this small group, we covenant together, with the help of God, to help one another grow in our understanding and application of what it means to love one another.

• Attending group meetings regularly whenever possible;

• Reading the chapter before each group session;

• Sharing our thoughts, goals, and struggles openly;

• Preserving confidentiality within the group; and

• Praying for one another.

Signed:_____

Date:_____

---

group. You can use the covenant included here, or adapt it to your group's goals. After you've discussed your covenant and agreed on it, have each group member sign a copy.

FOR DISCUSSION

1. What does it mean to you personally to be a member of the body of Christ? How have you been built up by other Christians?

2. Why are interdependence, humility, and unity so important for the body of Christ to function? In what specific ways have you seen each of these characteristics in your own church?

3. What would you consider to be the marks of Christian maturity? How is maturity developed? What is the relationship between "body maturity" and "personal maturity"?

4. How do the structures in your church foster "body function"? In what ways do they hinder this biblical process?

5. In what areas would you like to grow spiritually?

CLOSING

An important part of building community in a small group is praying for one another. In groups of two or three, share some specific prayer needs. Continue to pray specifically for the same people throughout the week.

For Next Time

1. Read chapter 2.
2. Pray for your prayer partners.
3. Follow through on the action steps you committed to in this session.

Chapter Two

Devoted to One Another

Be devoted to one another in brotherly love.

Romans 12:10a

The longer I am in the ministry and the more I encounter the devastating results of dysfunctional families, the more I am thankful for my own parents. Though they were virtually uneducated—Dad finished the sixth grade and Mom the eighth—they provided a secure environment for my three brothers and two sisters. Though they never had a course in child psychology and certainly made mistakes, they met our emotional needs far more significantly than many college-educated parents today.

As I reflect back on my childhood, I can honestly say I can't remember a moment when I was ever concerned that my parents wouldn't stay together. The thought never entered my mind. What a great heritage this is in view of the number of children today—even in Christian homes—who worry that either their dad or mom may have moved out when they come home from school.

Though my parents were never overly demonstrative, they were always physically affectionate toward all of us. Though we were geographically separated after I left home to attend college, we always hugged and kissed one another when I returned home to visit. This was simply an extension of what happened when I was growing up. It was natural for me to kiss them goodnight—every night—before I went to bed.

The most significant contribution to our lives was spiritual—which is certainly not separated from the way they met our psychological and physical needs. However, they taught us the true message of Christianity. They made sure we were in Sunday School regularly and I'll never forget Dad's family prayers—both before and after every meal. Furthermore, I'll always remember seeing Mom kneeling by her bed every night and praying for all of us.

Did this family environment make a difference when I became a Christian at age sixteen? Absolutely! I immediately felt at home in the family of God. The security I experienced in my family immediately transferred over to my brothers and sisters in Christ. I felt accepted and loved!

Furthermore, because I trusted my parents, I immediately trusted the leaders—my spiritual parents—in the church. And because I had learned to be affectionate with my family members, it was very natural for me to be affectionate within my new and larger "family."

What a great heritage! Though I didn't understand all of these dynamics until much later in my Christian experience, I came to realize how fortunate I really was! And, of course, this has become increasingly true as I interact with people on a regular basis who do not feel secure and safe among Christians because they have never felt secure and safe within the family unit.

THE FAMILY OF GOD

When Paul told the Roman Christians to *"be devoted to one another in brotherly love,"* he introduced us to another powerful metaphor to illustrate the church. The term *philadelphia*, translated "brotherly love," refers to family relationships. Applied to the church, Paul was referring to the love brothers and sisters in Christ should have for one another.

The term "brother" or "brothers" (*adelphos*), which in essence is part of the word *philadelphia*, is used by New Testament writers to refer to the "Christian family" approximately 220 times throughout the New Testament beginning with the Book of Acts.[1] The word literally means "from the same womb"—and in its generic form, includes both "brothers" and "sisters." It is distinctly a "family term." When it is applied to Christians, it means "fellow believers," "members of God's family," "brothers and sisters in Christ," and "members of God's household" (Eph. 2:19). It means we have all been "born again" into God's eternal family. We are vitally related to each other through a common heritage. God has "adopted" all of us "as [sons and daughters] through Jesus Christ" (Eph. 1:5).

Paul used the "body" metaphor to illustrate that Christians are "members of one another." It serves as a beautiful illustration to demonstrate *how* the church functions. Every believer is necessary and vitally important in God's plan. However, as with all analogies, the "human body" can go only so far in describing reality. The "family"—as God designed it to function—gives us an even greater appreciation of what a healthy church should be. This metaphor adds a dimension of warmth, tenderness, concern, and loyalty—in short, human emotion and devotion. Put another way, when Paul used the "body" metaphor, he used the *physical* aspects to illustrate the necessity of every member's participation in the church. But when he used the "family" metaphor, he was illustrating the *psychological* aspects of relational Christianity.

BAD NEWS! GOOD NEWS!

The family illustration introduces us to both "bad news" and "good news." The bad news is that children often grow up not knowing what it feels like to be accepted, loved unconditionally, and made to feel secure. They've not learned to trust others. They develop habits that are anything but Christian—learning to lie, cheat, and manipulate. Their values are based on relativism rather than on the absolute

---

[1]Following is the number of times the term "brother" or "brothers" is used in the New Testament, beginning in the Book of Acts: Acts (43); Romans (19); 1 Corinthians (37); 2 Corinthians (12); Galatians (10); Ephesians (3); Philippians (9); Colossians (5); 1 Thessalonians (19); 2 Thessalonians (9); 1 Timothy (3); 2 Timothy (1); Philemon (4); Hebrews (10); James (18); 1 Peter (11); 2 Peter (2); 1 John (17); 3 John (3); Revelation (5).

standards outlined in the Ten Commandments. They've learned to be selfish rather than benevolent and giving. Unfortunately, becoming a Christian doesn't automatically change these attitudes and actions that have been developed over a lengthy period of time. Consequently, when they join the "family of God," they have no idea what it means to be a loving, caring, trusting, and sincere brother or sister in Jesus Christ.

But this introduces us to the good news. God designed the church—the family of God—to be a "reparenting organism" to bring emotional and spiritual healing to people who have grown up in unhealthy families. Many people today need to *learn* for the first time how to love and care for others. They may never have experienced this kind of environment except in the church. When the church functions as God says it should, they can see it modeled in their new, extended family.

Think what this means to a young man who has never seen his father love his mother. Think what it means to a young woman who has never seen her mother love her father. A dynamic, healthy church may be the only place these young people will see what God really intended a marriage and family to be! This is indeed good news. However, there's more bad news! The world is filled with so-called Bible-believing churches that do not function as a family. Christians are often not "devoted to one another in brotherly love"—as Paul says we should be. In these churches, there is little warmth and caring among the members. Believers are not practicing the "one another" exhortations. Sadly, people who are converted to Christ often come out of one dysfunctional family to be exposed to another dysfunctional family. When this happens, God's plan for emotional and spiritual healing is thwarted. In fact, this can lead to disillusionment and spiritual devastation. We've just allowed Satan to score another victory.

A TWO-WAY STREET

Obviously, this whole process is a two-way street. Strong, mature families create strong, mature churches, and strong, mature churches create strong, mature families. However, when all is said and done, the "larger family" must take the lead—even if the church is made up of just a few strong families.

This is what happened in the New Testament. It didn't take a large group of households to create a strong family dynamic. Remember that where two or three are gathered, Jesus has promised to be present in a unique way (Matt. 18:20). Just so, when two or three families begin to function as God says they should, that church can have a powerful impact on people who need a good relational model.

I remember reading an article about a young couple who stood in line to buy Larry Flynt's autobiography and then to get his autograph. Standing beside them was their young daughter who was just three years old. To refresh your mind, Larry Flynt owns and edits *Hustler* magazine—one of the most vile, pornographic publications on the newsstands. He openly brags about the fact that one of his goals is to offend people.

A reporter approached this young girl's mother and asked her what she would do someday if her daughter eventually joined the many women who send in pornographic pictures of themselves in hopes of being displayed in the magazine. "When she grows up, she'll make her own choices," Mom said. "I'm real in favor of people making their own choices." This reporter went on to state that "this kind of thinking is behind a national coming-out party for a man who probably has ranked among America's Most Unwanted for two decades.[2]

Unfortunately, the story of this couple is not an exceptional reaction to moral trends in our society. Many parents no longer have any sense of responsibility to build into their children's lives the values that once made our society great. Rather than acknowledging this reality, we have given credit to a pornographer who blatantly violated what once was a strong national conscience that reflected the values of the Bible.

At the same time Flynt's book went on sale, Hollywood released the film entitled *The People Versus Larry Flynt*. Amazingly, this

---

[2] *The Dallas Morning News*, Tuesday, January 21, 1997.

movie immediately won two Golden Globes. "Apparently," this reporter continued, "you can lead a life of defiant debauchery . . . and still wind up a hero."[3]

Can the church bring healing and health to people who have been thoroughly secularized? The answer is a decided yes. It happened in the world of the New Testament, and it can happen in our own society that is still no match for the decadence in the Roman Empire. However, we will never help people become mature spiritually and psychologically if our church is not functioning as God says it should. We must "be devoted to one another in brotherly love."

PRACTICAL STEPS FOR DEVELOPING FAMILY RELATIONSHIPS IN YOUR CHURCH

Step 1

Showing affection and love to other Christians and treating them as brothers and sisters in Christ does not happen automatically. If it were automatic, we would not have so many exhortations to do so. Our first step must be to take seriously what the Bible says about brotherly love. Study carefully the following additional exhortations. Ask God to help you apply them in your life knowing this is part of walking in His will:

> Now about brotherly love we do not need to write to you, for you yourselves have been taught by God to love each other. And in fact, you do love all the brothers throughout Macedonia. Yet we urge you, brothers, to do so more and more (1 Thes. 4:9-10).

> Keep on loving each other as brothers. Do not forget to entertain strangers, for by so doing some people have entertained angels without knowing it. Remember those in prison as if you were their fellow prisoners, and those who are mistreated as if you yourselves were suffering (Heb. 13:1-3).

---

[3]*The Dallas Morning News*, Tuesday, January 21, 1997.

Now that you have purified yourselves by obeying the truth so that you have sincere love for your brothers, love one another deeply, from the heart. For you have been born again, not of perishable seed, but of imperishable, through the living and enduring word of God (1 Peter 1:22-23).

Finally, all of you, live in harmony with one another; be sympathetic, love as brothers, be compassionate and humble. Do not repay evil with evil or insult with insult, but with blessing, because to this you were called so that you may inherit a blessing (1 Peter 3:8-9).

For this very reason, make every effort to add to your faith goodness; and to goodness, knowledge; and to knowledge, self-control; and to self-control, perseverance; and to perseverance, godliness; and to godliness, brotherly kindness; and to brotherly kindness, love (2 Peter 1:5-7).

Step 2

Evaluate your attitudes and actions toward other members of your "Christian family." To what extent do you experience emotion and affection toward each fellow Christian? Note that Paul, in the context in which he exhorted Christians to "be devoted to one another in brotherly love," also exhorted that we "rejoice with those who rejoice" and "mourn with those who mourn" (Rom. 12:15). This, of course, involves emotion: deep feelings of joy as well as deep feelings of sadness.

Some Christians find it difficult to identify with other believers at the "feeling" level. There are reasons for this. And every Christian who finds it difficult to express emotion toward others should examine his life carefully, seeking to break the logjam that holds him back.

Consider the following questions:

1. Do I fear rejection?

Some individuals have been so deeply hurt by others they are afraid to express their feelings. They are not willing to take a chance on being hurt again. This, of course, is no excuse for not reaching out to others. We must work toward a mature perspective on human relationships. Christians must be vulnerable. And furthermore, most Christians to whom we reach out will not let us down. Don't let a bad experience rob you of God's best. Act on what you know to be the right thing to do.

Nancy had been rejected by her father. Nothing she did seemed to please him, especially when she couldn't maintain a B average in high school. She withdrew from making further attempts to win his approval. This attitude carried over into her adult life. She seemed continually withdrawn. She couldn't risk the chance of being rejected again, so she never attempted those creative activities that would win recognition.

2. Have I had a poor family background?

Some people grow up in homes where physical affection and love toward other family members are seldom or perhaps never expressed. For example, Mary grew up in a home where family members rarely demonstrated affection. This does not mean they didn't love each other. They just didn't show it outwardly or with emotion. Her husband Bill's experience was just the opposite. Consequently, he has always found it easy to physically express affection to others. Mary, however, had to learn this process as an adult—which was often difficult, but she has done well. But, of course, it took time.

When people have been taught by example and practice to keep their feelings inside and never to express them, this attitude usually carries over in dealing with members of the family of God. It takes time to reverse such behavioral patterns.

Some Christians also have difficulty expressing emotions to God because of negative experiences in the home—particularly with an earthly father. These emotions are very easily transferred to the Heavenly Father—as well as to other members of the body of Christ.

I remember attempting to lead a young woman to Christ. She knew she had sinned and needed a Savior. Consequently, I asked her to pray to God and to invite Jesus Christ to come into her heart and life. I began the prayer asking her to repeat after me. "Heavenly Father," I said—and then paused. There was no response. I thought she misunderstood, so I repeated the opening thought—"Heavenly Father." Again, I paused and again there was silence.

I then asked this young woman if there was something wrong. "Yes," she replied. "I can't use that word"—meaning the word "father." She then went on to explain that her earthly father had sexually abused her as a young child.

I quickly changed my opening words to "O God." She had no problem verbalizing these words, and we continued on from there.

How sad! But how true! How we function as earthly fathers forms our children's view of their Heavenly Father. This is an awesome reality.

If this illustration represents your situation—even a little bit—seek help from a fellow Christian you trust. Find someone who will not condemn you but will listen to you with sympathy and concern. Share your deepest and innermost feelings. Pray together.

3. Am I basically angry and resentful?

Some Christians are controlled by deep feelings of anger and resentment toward other people. They are usually individuals who have repressed these feelings in early childhood. They find it very difficult to express positive emotions even toward fellow Christians.

Some people who have been severely repressed in childhood, and who have experienced unusual trauma, may need professional counsel. This kind of problem is not so much spiritual, but psychological, in its roots.

4. Do I spend most of my time thinking about myself?

Some Christians are very selfish and self-centered. They think only about themselves. They couldn't care less about their brothers and sisters in Christ. Naturally, they find it difficult to express "brotherly love."

This selfish attitude is often expressed in their prayers. Larry discovered how often he pleaded with God to give him things. Almost every prayer centered on Larry's desires for himself. Fortunately, he noticed how others in the church spent considerable time praying for those with greater needs. He decided to put others on the top of his prayer list. Life soon took on new meaning.

Step 3

If you identify with any of the difficulties above, seek help from a fellow member of the body of Christ who is mature and someone you trust. Whatever step you take, begin to act immediately on what you know to be God's will. For example, if you have difficulty telling a fellow Christian you love him, begin to act on what you know is the right thing to do. Don't wait until you feel like it! Start by doing something that is not overly threatening emotionally—sharing with that person a gift, a note of appreciation, an invitation to dinner. Frequently, feelings begin to follow actions—particularly when we are emotionally rewarded and appreciated for our acts of kindness. Expressing love in a tangible way will help you to eventually develop feelings of love that you can share verbally.

If you've been deeply hurt and frustrated or repressed, don't allow yourself to withdraw. You'll only become more disillusioned. Your problems will get worse. Most people interpret someone with reserved behavior as someone who needs little love or attention. Worse yet, they think such a person really doesn't want to be involved with other people. As a result, the person who withdraws quickly becomes isolated from those who could offer the greatest help.

THE FAMILY OF GOD

You will notice we say brother and sister 'round here—
It's because we're a family and these folks are so dear.
When one has a heartache we all share the tears
And rejoice in each vict'ry in this family so dear.

From the door of an orph'nage to the house of the king,
No longer an outcast, a new song I sing.

From rags unto riches, from the weak to the strong,
I'm not worthy to be here, but praise God, I belong.

CHORUS:
I'm so glad I'm a part of the family of God;
I've been washed in the fountain, cleansed by the blood;
Joint heirs with Jesus as we travel this sod,
For I'm part of the family, the family of God.[4]

DISCUSSION GUIDE FOR SMALL GROUPS

OPENING

Have each person share his or her responses to these questions:

What was your family like when you were growing up?
What dreams do you have for your family now?
When did you first realize what it meant to be part of the family of God?

FOR DISCUSSION

1. What would a church look like that truly functioned as the family of God? In what ways have you seen your church function as the family of God?

2. Read the Scripture passages listed under Step 1 for developing family relationships in your church. If your small group were to take seriously those exhortations, how would it impact this group? How might it impact the church?

3. Answer the following questions regarding feelings of rejection:

How does fear of rejection hinder someone from "being devoted to one another"?

How can a person overcome the fear of rejection?
How can others help someone who fears rejection?
What might indicate that a person is afraid of being rejected?
When do you feel most at risk for being rejected?

4. What is the relationship between a person's family background and the way that person relates to the church "family"? What are your own emotional reactions to words like "father" or "brother"?

5. What does your prayer life say about your level of concern for members of your church family? Make a list of prayer concerns relating to others in your church family that you can pray about individually and as a group.

CLOSING

In groups of two or three, share your personal reaction to the roadblocks to brotherly love listed in this chapter. Do you have past hurts that prevent you from offering or experiencing love in the family of God? Or do you perhaps know someone who needs special attention to experience that love? What steps can you take to act on what you know to be in God's will? After sharing your concerns in your group of two or three, pray for one another's concerns.

For Next Time

1. Read chapter 3.
2. Pray for the needs of your church family that you listed in this group session.
3. Continue to pray for the concerns of your small group members.
4. Take one of the steps you identified as part of God's will.

Chapter Three

Honor One Another

Honor one another above yourselves.

Romans 12:10

I have a friend—a worship leader and a pianist extraordinaire. His name is Brent Tallent, which brings a lot of interesting comments in view of his musical accomplishments.

Brent tells a rather humorous story about himself—which sets the stage beautifully for our study on this "one another" that states—"Honor one another above yourselves" (Rom. 12:10).

When Brent was just a young man, a very well-known soloist came to his church, and he had the privilege of serving as her accompanist. He was excited, seeing this as an opportunity to demonstrate his skills at the keyboard. During the rehearsal, he proceeded to run his fingers up and down the keyboard in Liberace style while she sang the first stanza of her song.

Following this initial verse, she stopped, looked at my friend, and said with a smile—"You know, Brent, I really make a wonderful accompanist for you!"

The light went on! Suddenly Brent saw what he had done! He was to be the accompanist! He was to support a soloist—never overshadowing and calling attention to his own skills. In short, he was to do everything he could to make *her* "look and sound good"!

When I heard this story, I quickly recognized a powerful metaphor that illustrates what it really means to honor others above ourselves. You see every Christian is to be "an accompanist" to every other Christian. We're all to make *one another* "look and sound good"!

Incidentally, Brent never forgot that lesson. Today, though a great soloist in his own right, he is one of the finest accompanists I know. He knows how "to honor others" at the keyboard—and does it beautifully. As I listen to him play, I'll never forget the metaphor. My responsibility as a Christian—and yours too—is to make others "look and sound good." When we do, we'll be honoring others above ourselves!

CHRIST'S SUPREME EXAMPLE

Jesus Christ, when He walked on earth, set the supreme example in honoring others above Himself. On one occasion, a short time before His death, He taught the disciples a powerful truth, which is also a great metaphor. At an evening meal together, Jesus—knowing full well "that the Father had put all things under his power, and that he had come from God and was returning to God"—filled a basin with water and stooped to wash His disciples' feet. After He had finished the task, He shared with them a lesson I'm sure they never forgot.

"Do you understand," He asked, "what I have done for you?" Then He went on to answer His own question. "You call me 'Teacher' and 'Lord,' and rightly so, for that is what I am. Now that I, your Lord and Teacher, have washed your feet, you also should wash one another's feet. I have set you an example that you should do as I have done for you" (John 13:12-15).

It's my opinion that some Christians confuse principle and pattern in this story, and believe that Jesus is teaching us to actually wash one another's feet in today's culture. I certainly respect and admire Christians who practice this ancient custom as well as their desire to be obedient to Christ. There is certainly freedom in Christ for any Christian to wash another Christian's feet. In fact, it can be a powerful example.

A MARK OF TRUE HUMILITY!

I'll never forget attending the pastors' conference in Atlanta, Georgia, sponsored by Promise Keepers. Over forty thousand ministers gathered to worship together and to be challenged to be faithful to our calling in Christ. Bishop Wellington Boone was preaching. Suddenly, he stopped and turned to Tony Evans—a fellow pastor—who was seated on the platform. "Tony," he said, "I'm willing to wash your feet in order to serve you."

In a matter of minutes, something very spontaneous happened. Several men in the audience placed a makeshift container on the platform and filled it with a few bottles of water. They gave Wellington Boone a piece of cloth—probably some kind of T-shirt. He knelt before Tony Evans, removed his shoes and socks, and began washing his feet—all the time telling this brother in Christ that he loved him and wanted to serve him as a fellow pastor. I'll never forget that experience. This was a true mark of humility—and captured what Jesus had in mind when He told his disciples to serve and love one another (John 13:12-15, 34-35).

A MARK OF TRUE SERVANTHOOD!

Let me share another contemporary experience. A group of teenagers from our church went on a wilderness trip for several days in the Colorado mountains. On the last day, as they reached the end of this arduous journey, they sat by a cool mountain stream, removed their shoes from their tired—and in most instances—bruised and hurting feet. At that moment, one of the pastors who guided these young people on this expedition suggested that they serve one another by washing each other's feet, and to share words of love and appreciation. It was a powerful experience—and one that certainly met the need at the moment, and also turned a "cultural necessity" into an opportunity to practice Jesus' exhortation to serve others.

Whatever our view on foot washing, we must never forget the message and principle Jesus was teaching. Though cultures change, though modes of transportation have evolved, and though most of us usually walk on sidewalks with shoes on our feet rather than sandals on dirty, dusty roads—there is one thing that has not changed! Paul confirmed this when he said that we as Christians are to "honor one another above ourselves." This is what Jesus was illustrating in the foot-washing episode.

A MARK OF TRUE HONOR!

On another occasion, Jesus spelled out this truth even more clearly. He took the religious leaders to task for their pride and arrogance. "Everything they do is done for men to see," He said. "They love *the place of honor* at banquets and *the most important seats* in the synagogues; they love to be greeted in the marketplaces and to have men call them 'Rabbi.'"

Then Jesus turned to His disciples and drove home the lesson they had to learn if they were to be mature men of God who could be used in His service: "The greatest among you will be your servant. For whoever exalts himself will be humbled, and whoever humbles himself will be exalted" (Matt. 23:5-12).

I remember being invited on one occasion to speak at a national conference sponsored by the Fellowship of Christian Airline Personnel (FCAP). This Christian organization is attended by anyone who works in the airline industry—from pilots and flight attendants to the ground crews that refuel planes and transport baggage.

When I arrived at the conference center, I was greeted by none other than the pilots who had flown for major airlines for years. The man who met me and who carried my bags was a captain who flew L1011s—huge jumbo jets. I then noticed when other airline personnel arrived for the conference, these same distinguished pilots also greeted these people—no matter what their position in the industry—and carried their bags to their rooms. I thought to myself—"What a gesture of true servanthood and honor!" And what an example of what Jesus had in mind when He said, "The greatest among you will be your servant"!

PAUL'S DYNAMIC APPLICATION

The Apostle Paul, though he never sat at the feet of Christ while He taught on earth, learned to honor others. He applied this truth in his own life, and he taught others to do the same. Thus he wrote to the Philippians: "Your attitude should be the same as that of Christ Jesus" (Phil. 2:5).

What was that attitude? Paul carefully spelled it out! Christ demonstrated toward all humankind the greatest act of *unselfishness, humility,* and *self-sacrifice* ever known in the universe:

> Who, being in very nature God, did not consider equality with God something to be grasped, but made himself nothing, taking the very nature of a servant, being made in human likeness. And being found in appearance as a man, He humbled himself and became obedient to death—even death on a cross! (Phil. 2:6-8)

The result of Christ's act of love and submission brought to Himself in essence the very same result He promised His disciples if they would "honor others above themselves"—exaltation! This is what God did for Jesus Christ:

> Therefore God exalted him to the highest place and gave him the name that is above every name, that at the name of Jesus every knee should bow, in heaven and on earth and under the earth, and every tongue confess that Jesus Christ is Lord, to the glory of God the Father (Phil. 2:9-11).

Our personal exaltation will always be different from that of Christ's. Nevertheless, God will exalt Christians who truly honor others above themselves. It may not be immediate, but it will happen—if not on earth, throughout all eternity, where it will really count. Jesus Himself taught that "many who are first will be last, and many who are last will be first" (Matt. 19:30).

To make sure the Philippians understood what he meant by imitating Christ's attitudes and actions, he introduced this whole paragraph about Christ's act of humility and unselfishness by saying:

> Do nothing out of selfish ambition or vain conceit, but in

humility consider others better than yourselves. Each of you should look not only to your own interests, but also to the interests of others (Phil. 2:3-4).

Don't misunderstand! The Bible doesn't teach that we should not have our own interests. That would be impossible. The very nature of life—rearing a family, making a living, competing in the workplace, and taking time for ourselves—demands that we look after our own interests. However, the Bible does teach that we should "look *not only*" to our "own interests, but also to the interests of others." It teaches us that we should "consider others better than ourselves." We should not be motivated by self-centered motives and pride ("vain conceit"). Our goal should be to honor Jesus Christ first, others second, and ourselves third. If we do, we will be honored in due time. As Jesus said, we cannot lose our lives without finding them again (Matt. 10:39).

PRACTICAL STEPS FOR APPLYING THIS PRINCIPLE TODAY

Step 1

Take a careful look at your "honoring others" quotient!

The following questions will help you:

How many situations can you recall where you purposely attempted to honor someone above yourself?

What about yesterday? Last week? Last month?

In what ways did you reflect sincere appreciation for the other person?

At this point, be careful! We've all met "backslappers." They're opportunists—using the opportunity to exalt others as a means to exalt themselves. This is their ultimate goal. They're willing to "scratch our backs" if we'll "scratch theirs." Someone has said that they've revised the "Golden Rule"—to "Do unto others so they will do for you." This is definitely not what Paul had in mind when he told us to "honor one another above ourselves."

Usually this kind of tactic backfires. It radiates insincerity. In fact, if these people don't get immediate results, they often reverse their field. Rather than truly "building others up," they will start "putting those people down." If we're truly honoring others, we'll never allow ourselves to become vindictive if they don't respond.

Step 2

Don't forget to honor those who have helped you become what you are!

As a professor and pastor, I've helped train many young people—young men particularly. Some I've helped in very significant ways. Because of my own position, I've opened doors of opportunity through telephone calls or letters of recommendation. At times, I've actually made appointments with key people, and have personally built bridges for them.

Unfortunately, some of these young men have "walked through these doors" and have never looked back over their shoulder and even said thanks. In fact, when they tell their own success stories, you never hear them mention those who helped them get where they are!

It's tempting at times to become extremely disappointed in these individuals—especially when they are in full-time ministry. They somehow have conveniently "forgotten" who helped them, who believed in them, and who opened the doors of opportunity. This has not only happened to me personally, but to other Christian leaders I know.

The facts are that all of us have gotten where we are with the help of others. I know this is true in my own life. I will be forever grateful to a professor at Moody Bible Institute named Harold Garner who took a personal interest in me. He believed in me when I didn't believe in myself. He took me on trips so I could observe him speaking at various conferences and to listen in when he was interacting with people. He gave me my first opportunity to speak and share in one of those conferences. I wrote and published my first article because he recommended me. I had my first significant ministry experience because he built the bridge. Eventually, I became a faculty member at Moody Bible Institute because he also recommended me!

I've tried hard never to "practice what I'm preaching" in this chapter—to never allow myself to forget what he did for me. I made it a point to thank him periodically while he was still living—though I wish I had done so more often. I must admit there were times when I was tempted to "honor myself" rather than him—to take credit for things that I knew I would not be doing if it were not for what he did for me. However, when that happened, I attempted to get back on track and give credit where credit is due. I'll be forever grateful to this man the rest of my life—and in eternity. He'll definitely be rewarded for what I've been able to contribute to God's kingdom—perhaps more so than me.

Let me say it again! Don't forget those who have helped you become what you are! When was the last time you thanked them?

Step 3

If it is difficult for you to compliment others and to enjoy their successes, take a close look at your own personality.

The following checkpoints will help:

1. Some people cannot compliment others and enjoy their success because they have always been the center of attention themselves.

For example, Jane is an only child and always had everything she wanted. Over the years she became self-centered. Now as an adult, she finds it very difficult to even compliment her husband. Rather, she tends to "compete" with him. Unfortunately, her problem is about to destroy her marriage.

This, of course, represents a serious spiritual and emotional problem and reflects immaturity. This was the problem with the Corinthians. If this is your problem, confess your sin and reprogram your life. Memorize Philippians 2:3-4, and meditate on these exhortations every day.

Every time you're tempted to "hog the show," quote those verses to yourself. Ask God to bring them to your memory when you find yourself being tempted.

2. Some people have difficulty complimenting and honoring

others because they are insecure.

In these situations, the results are often the same, but the emotional dynamics are different. These people, rather than being purely self-centered, don't feel good about themselves. They have difficulty "honoring others" because they feel in need of honor themselves. In fact, they are the kind of people who can never get enough honor and attention. They feed on it; they gorge themselves—and still cry out for more! Even after all this, they often complain no one pays attention to them. This is also a form of self-centeredness, but the motivation is different from those who are purely selfish.

For example, Tom is that kind of person. As a child he was always put down. His parents were so busy trying to get attention from each other they failed to give any to Tom. Consequently, he grew up an insecure person. Now he finds within himself an insatiable desire for recognition and attention. And he'll do almost anything to get it.

Tom has a psychological problem as well as a spiritual one. In their past, people like him were not given enough love and attention. Consequently, they have developed a spongelike personality. They can't seem to give. They always want to receive. Can you identify?

This kind of person needs insight, understanding, and help from others. He needs to recognize the necessity of reprogramming his mind and emotions. In addition to memorizing Scripture (such as Phil. 2:3-4), he needs loving counsel blended with direct confrontation regarding his patterns of behavior.

If either of these two problems describe your behavior, begin today to seek help from another mature member of Christ's church. Don't disobey God another day (no matter what the cause of your problem). If you continue, you'll rob yourself of the blessing that will come if you truly "honor others above yourself."

Remember, you can never lose by sincerely honoring others. God will not forget, and neither will those you honor.

ETERNAL LIFE

Lord, make me an instrument of your peace,
Where there is hatred, let me sow love—

Where there is injury, pardon—
Where there is doubt, faith—
Where there is despair, hope—
Where there is darkness, light—
Where there is sadness, joy.

O Divine Master, grant that I may not so much seek
To be consoled—as to console,
To be understood—as to understand,
To be loved—as to love,
For
It is in giving that we receive,
It is in pardoning that we are pardoned,
It is in dying that we are born to eternal life.

St. Francis of Assisi

DISCUSSION GUIDE FOR SMALL GROUPS

OPENING (Choose one)

1. Have each person share his or her responses to these questions:

What compliment or honor have you received that meant the most to you? Why?

2. Pass around a basin of water and a towel. Have each person wash the feet of the person next to him or her. Then share your responses to these questions:

How did you feel when the person was washing your feet?

What were you thinking when you were washing someone else's feet?

When was the last time someone symbolically washed your feet? What did he or she do and what did that experience mean to you?

FOR DISCUSSION

1. Read John 13:1-17. If you had been one of the disciples whose feet Jesus washed, how do you think you would have responded? How might that experience have affected your relationship to the other disciples? If Jesus were to come and give that same example to your group today, what action might He take instead of washing your feet?

2. What are some practical ways we can apply the principle of serving and honoring that emerges from Jesus' foot-washing example? In our own small group? In our church? In the greater community? Which of those actions are you personally willing to take?

3. Read Philippians 2:3. What is the relationship between having a healthy self-esteem and "considering others better than yourself"? How does Philippians 2:5-11 deepen your understanding of that relationship?

4. Did you identify with any of the problems mentioned in "Practical Steps for Applying This Principle Today"? Share your struggles openly with the group and pray for one another. (Option: you may prefer to share in smaller groups of three or four people.)

5. What is the next step you need to take in honoring one another?

CLOSING

Take some time to honor and affirm one another for the strengths God has given each person. Use one of these options, or create your own:

1. Have each person sit in the center of the circle while the other group members complete this sentence: One thing I admire about you is . . .

2. Go around the circle, having each person complete the above sentence to the person on his or her right.

3. Have each person choose one of the following awards for every other person in the group. Then have each person take turns sitting in the center of the group while the other members tell what award they have chosen for that person.

Nobel Peace Prize: for the person who helps us stay on good terms even when we disagree.

Golden Globe Award: for the person who helps us see beyond ourselves to the big picture.

Stanley Cup: for the person who knows how to use teamwork to keep us moving toward the goal.

Indy 500 Trophy: for the person who is raring to go and keeps us moving.

Oscar: for the person who acts out what we are learning.

Other:

For Next Time

1. Read chapter 4.
2. Memorize Philippians 2:3-4.
3. Choose one way you are going to honor someone this week. Come prepared to share what you have done.

Chapter Four

Be of the Same Mind
with One Another

Now may the God who gives perseverance and encouragement grant you to be of the same mind with one another according to Christ Jesus.

Romans 15:5, NASB

I love to ski, and one of my favorite mountains in Colorado is Crested Butte. It was the end of the day, and I came off the mountain, got on the bus, and was waiting to return to the lodge.

It had been a beautiful day! Mother Nature had dropped a foot of fresh snow the day before and the grooming crews had worked all night getting the slopes ready for the next day. And when the day dawned, the sun came up and shone all day long. The skiing conditions were perfect.

As I sat on the bus, reflecting on the great time I had that day, a man got on the bus carrying a young woman. She must have been in her early teens and I quickly concluded he must have been her father. My initial thoughts were that she had hurt herself. But then I noticed something else was wrong. As she sat in the seat next to the aisle, the man who had carried her onto the bus put his arm around her and held her upright. If he hadn't, she would have fallen to the floor. I also noticed that she tried to talk and gesture with her arms but the words that came out were garbled and her arms were difficult to control. I then saw she had a serious problem with coordination. There wasn't anything wrong with her intelligence and she was definitely happy—though her smile contorted when she tried to share her excitement about the day.

Sadly, this woman represented those human tragedies where the brain sends signals to various parts of the body, but they don't respond properly. She was definitely physically challenged. People often use the word "spastic" to describe this condition—which in itself is not a complimentary word. It was obvious, however, that in spite of her handicaps, she had enjoyed the day—perhaps strapped in a sled.

As I sat and watched, I realized how fortunate I was to be coordinated. In fact, I'd skied all day long, making turns and negotiating moguls, taking for granted that my legs and arms would respond properly to the signals from my brain.

But as I sat and reflected, I thought of another tragedy—in many respects, a much greater tragedy. I thought of all of the "spastic churches" that exist in the world today—churches where Jesus Christ the Head sends signals to various members of His body, but they do not respond properly. In fact, they do just the opposite of what the Lord has stated. Consequently, the church lacks unity and coordination. It's filled with carnality—and divisions. The church in Corinth was this kind of body of believers. "You are still worldly," Paul wrote. "For since there is jealousy and quarreling among you, are you not worldly? Are you not acting like mere men? [or like non-Christians]" (1 Cor. 3:3).

CHRIST'S PRAYER FOR UNITY

In Christ's prayer to the Father recorded in John 17, He made direct reference to at least four major elements in the incomparable message of Christianity—salvation (17:1-3); the Incarnation (17:4-6); sanctification (17:17-19); and glorification (17:24). Central in this beautiful and profound prayer is one major request—that Christ's disciples (and Christians of all time) might experience unity and oneness. "Holy Father," prayed Jesus, "protect them by the power of your name—the name you gave me—so *that they may be one as We are one*" (John 17:11).

Later, Jesus amplified this request:

> My prayer is not for them alone. I pray also for those who will believe in me through their message [believers of all time], that all of them may be one, Father, just as you are in me and I am in you. May they also be in us so that the world may believe that you have sent me. I have given them the glory that you gave me, that they may be one as we are one: I in them and you in me. May they be brought to complete unity to let the world know that you sent me and have loved them even as you have loved me (John 17:20-23).

THE ESSENCE OF CHRISTIANITY

Jesus Christ's primary concern for His church stands out boldly in this prayer. It is a visible unity—a oneness—that reveals the very essence of the Christian Gospel. That essence comprises the fact "that God was reconciling the world to himself in Christ" (2 Cor. 5:19). Jesus was indeed God in the flesh. He was (and is) one with the Father. And oneness in Christ's body in some miraculous and marvelous way reveals that Christ is indeed God. If He had not been God, there could have been no plan of salvation. Christianity would be just another man-made religion.

This is why Satan's strategy throughout church history has been to destroy unity in Christ's body. This makes a lot of sense from Satan's point of view. If he can destroy unity, he has eliminated the most powerful means to communicate that Jesus Christ is God. When that message is obliterated or even blurred, people are doomed to eternal despair. No one can come to know God apart from coming to know Jesus Christ, the Son of God (John 14:6; 20:30-31).

A POWERFUL MIRACLE

When Christ was on earth, He worked miracles to convince men He was God. When He went back to heaven, He left His church to communicate that truth. And the ingredient in the church that convinces non-Christians that Jesus is God is unity—being of "the same mind with one another." This, too, represents a miracle, because people everywhere tend toward disunity. History flows with lack of harmony among humankind. Wars have been the norm—the standard for human behavior. When non-Christians see true unity and true oneness, their hearts cry out to be a part of that kind of love.

I'll never forget an experience I had in the first Fellowship Bible Church. Unknown to me, a young couple that was visiting for the first time did not believe that Jesus Christ was God in the flesh. However, they sat and listened intently to me teach the Scriptures and also stayed for the second part of our service—a time of open sharing. I closed the service with a silent invitation—still not knowing they were there—giving everyone an opportunity to quietly invite the Lord Jesus Christ into their lives as Savior. I found out later they made that decision.

But I also discovered something else. It was not my message per se that God used to bring them to faith in Christ. Rather, it was the second part of the service where the body of Christ functioned in love and unity. They shared later that they opened their hearts to the Gospel when they saw believers loving one another, honoring one another, and praying for each other's needs. In short, they saw a functioning, loving body of believers. They saw a oneness in Christ. This was the "miracle" that the Holy Spirit used to open their hearts to the incarnational message I was teaching and preaching. This is what Jesus Christ prayed for and what the late Dr. Francis Schaeffer called "the final apologetic."

Think for a moment what happened! This couple came into the service unbelievers—not only in the sense that they had not received the Lord Jesus Christ as Savior. They did not even believe He was the "Word become flesh" (John 1:14). However, a couple of hours later they walked out new believers. How easy it would be for me—and others—to conclude it was my message alone and the invitation to respond that brought them to Christ, when in reality it was an answer to Jesus' prayer—that we might "be brought to complete unity to let the world know" that God had sent Jesus

Christ into this world because of His love for all mankind (17:23).

Over the years as I've had the privilege of leading people to Christ, I've seen this happen frequently. It's what I like to call "body evangelism." When we're "of the same mind with one another," the Holy Spirit causes the message to come alive in the hearts of unbelievers. Though I may have led them to make a decision for Christ, in reality the "whole church" led them to faith in Christ. This is what God intended to happen on a regular basis.

PAUL'S PRAYER FOR UNITY

It's interesting that Paul's elaboration "to be of the same mind with one another" is also in the form of a prayer. In this sense, he was following Jesus' example. Note also that prior to this "one another" prayer, Paul issued two more "one another" exhortations that set the stage for this prayer for unity.

Don't "Judge One Another"

First, Paul told these believers not to "judge one another," but rather, to determine "not to put any stumbling block or obstacle" in a brother's way (Rom. 14:3). In other words, even if we feel we have freedom to do certain things that do not violate the will of God, the law of love should cause us to avoid any behavior that may cause another brother or sister to stumble and fall into sin.

"BUILD UP ONE ANOTHER"

Second, Paul preceded his prayer for unity and one-mindedness with another "one another" exhortation—to "pursue the things which make for peace and the *building up of one another*" (14:19, NASB).[1] Paul gave the same basic exhortation to the Ephesians when he told them to "make every effort to keep the unity of the Spirit through the bond of peace" (Eph. 4:3).

It's true that when we become Christians, we are one in Christ. This is how God sees us—just as He sees a man and wife who come

---

[1] In this instance, the NIV translates *allelon* as "mutual edification"—which is an excellent interpretation of what it really means to "build up one another."

together in an intimate relationship as being "one flesh" (5:31). However, all Christians—including husbands and wives—do not reflect this unity in all aspects of their lives unless they do everything possible to make it happen.

Again, we need divine resources to enable us to "pursue" this unity. It will not happen automatically. It takes work and effort to be the kind of people God wants us to be. That's why Jesus, prior to His prayer for unity, told His disciples in no uncertain terms to "love one another" as He had just loved them (John 13:33-34). In this situation, this meant humbling themselves, walking across the room, picking up a towel and a basin of water, and washing one another's feet.

SATAN'S PRIMARY STRATEGY

Paul's prayer for one-mindedness and unity underscores and emphasizes why Satan's primary strategy throughout church history has been to destroy unity among Bible-believing Christians. He wants to drive people away from Christ. But this is also why Satan has tried to create a sense of unity among false religions—particularly those that deny the deity of Christ.

As I was discussing this great truth one day, I remember talking to a missionary to the Mormons. He told me about a young man who had graduated from a well-known evangelical Bible institute with plans to go to the mission field under the auspices of a well-known mission. However, after graduating and before he went to the mission field, he decided to visit a Mormon community. He wanted to see how they operated—how they did their mission work. He simply wanted to see what he could learn.

Surprisingly, after being exposed to Mormonism, this young man who professed to believe that Jesus Christ was God—decided to become a Mormon and to join a religious community that openly denies that Jesus Christ came in the flesh and was One with God. When he was asked why he converted to Mormonism, this young man replied quickly and to the point. He felt he had seen and sensed more love and unity in the Mormon church than he had ever seen in an evangelical Bible-believing church that taught that

Jesus Christ was God and that the only way to heaven was to accept the Lord Jesus Christ as personal Savior.

We can argue all we want that what he experienced was not true Christian love. However, in his words, he saw care and concern that ought to characterize true Christians. As Jesus said, sometimes the "people of this world" demonstrate more wisdom "than the people of the light" (Luke 16:8).

In another case, one young woman whose parents attended our church was attracted to Sun Myung Moon's Unification Church. She too felt love, acceptance, and a sense of oneness of purpose among these people—something she evidently did not sense in her home or in the church she had attended from her childhood. No amount of "sound doctrine" could convince her that these people were in violation of Scripture. When she visited our church with her parents, we tried to convince her of the doctrinal error in the Unification Church. However, having her emotional needs met was far more important to her than intellectual arguments regarding the deity of Christ.

Both of these stories illustrate the power Satan has in blinding people to the most basic truth in all of Christianity. If Christ were not God, He never could have been the perfect sacrifice on the cross. The Incarnation is the essence of the Gospel (2 Cor. 5:18-19).

What an incredible twofold strategy! On the one hand, Satan tries to destroy love and unity in churches that truly believe in the deity of Jesus Christ. On the other hand, he attempts to simulate love and unity in churches and groups that deny the deity of Christ. What better way to drive people away from the Gospel. On the one hand, people are repulsed by disunity among those people who have the truth, and on the other hand, they are attracted to groups that simulate unity but who do not believe the truth.

SATAN CAN BE DEFEATED

Fortunately, God gave us a strategy for defeating Satan. We can be "of the same mind with one another" and see the results. Let me share two more powerful illustrations of what can happen when we practice this "one another" exhortation. Both happened to me personally when I was visiting two different South American countries.

A PRIMITIVE SETTING

On one occasion, I had an opportunity to minister to a group of missionaries in Quito, Ecuador. They had gathered for their annual conference for spiritual refreshment and encouragement.

Prior to the beginning of the conference, I spoke with one of the veteran couples who had ministered in that area of the world for many years, particularly to a large Ecuadorian Indian tribe. Without knowing the subject I was going to speak on, they shared with me that, at a particular point in time in their ministry, they experienced an unusual outpouring of the Holy Spirit. Literally thousands of these Indians responded to the Gospel and put their faith in Jesus Christ for salvation.

I was naturally intrigued with their encouraging story and I asked them if there was any particular thing they could point to that may have precipitated this unusual spiritual response. They both thought about that question for a moment—and then the wife responded by saying, "Yes! There was something very significant that happened! And once that happened," she continued, "it was then that we saw this unusual response to the Gospel message."

Unknown to this couple, they shared an experience that was directly related to one of the messages I had planned for the whole group of missionaries gathered at this annual conference. My two primary texts for that message that day came from Jesus' exhortations to His disciples to "love one another" (John 13:34-35) and from His prayer for unity in John 17.

You see, this couple had been a part of a preaching team for many years that had ministered to this large South American Indian tribe. However, for a lengthy period of time, there had been disunity in the rather large group of missionaries working among this tribe. And then God's Holy Spirit did a special work of grace in the hearts of these missionaries. They confessed their faults to one another and asked forgiveness. Unity was restored, and the love among these people was very strong and obvious to the people to whom they had been ministering. Consequently, the Holy Spirit worked in the lives of the Indians who had been resistant to the Gospel. Literally thousands put their faith in Jesus Christ for salvation. You see, this was an answer to Jesus' prayer and an illustration of what Paul had in mind with his "one another" exhortation to be "of the same mind with one another."

A CULTURED ENVIRONMENT

My second experience happened in Brazil. I have a very close friend, Jim Petersen, who ministered in this country with The Navigators for over 25 years. He and his wife, Marge, worked primarily with secular people, many of whom were Marxists and agnostics. They were highly educated people—doctors, lawyers, architects, etc. Jim's approach again and again was to get these people to study the Scriptures, simply to see what the Bible says. Though it took time to bring people to faith in Christ, once decisions were made, they resulted from a comprehensive knowledge of God's truth. Furthermore, it was the Holy Spirit, the divine author of Scripture, who enabled these people to believe (1 Cor. 12:3).

One of these individuals was Mario Nitche, who classified himself as an atheist. When Jim met Mario, he was attending a meeting where a Christian psychologist from the United States was speaking. Jim—who was relatively new on the field—was interpreting Portuguese for the guest speaker, and after the lecture, Mario approached him with some questions. Sensing Mario's inquisitive mind as well as his atheistic position, Jim asked him if he would like to study the Bible just to see what it says. Mario agreed.

They began to meet on a regular basis to study the Book of Romans. As they started reading in chapter 1, they came to the name "Jesus Christ." At that point, Mario informed Jim that he did not believe in Jesus Christ, even as a historical person. "That's all right," Jim replied. "Let's call him 'X.' Let's just see what Paul says."

Mario agreed to this arrangement and they went on. Next, they came to the word "God." Again, Mario objected. He did not believe in God. And again, they agreed to substitute the letter "X" for God. And so, they continued meeting together weekly—off and on—for a period of four years. Finally, Mario became a believer.

When I met Mario, he had been a Christian for many years. I had the opportunity to be in his home. Being aware of his story, I asked Mario what caused him to continue to meet with Jim for four years to study a book he did not believe contained the truth. He paused for a moment and then responded very quickly and without equivocation. He said, "It was definitely the love relationship I saw between Jim and his wife, Marge. It was the way they treated their children. And it was the love and unity developed in that family. That," he said, "is why I continued to study the Bible. I wanted what they had and I knew there had to be a relationship between what I saw in their family life and what they all believed the Bible taught."

In the Bible, the family is the church in miniature. Here we see that Paul's prayer for unity applies not only to the church family, but to every single family unit that is a part of the church. We can say the same about all of the other "one another" exhortations in this study. In fact, they apply *wherever* we have Christian relationships.

THE JERUSALEM CHURCH — A DYNAMIC EXAMPLE

Immediately following Christ's return to heaven, the church in Jerusalem emerged as a direct answer to Jesus' prayer. Their unity was profound. Luke recorded, "And day by day *continuing with one mind* in the temple, and breaking bread from house to house, they were taking their meals together with gladness and sincerity of heart" (Acts 2:46, NASB). And later Luke added, "All the believers were *one in heart and mind*" (Acts 4:32).

This does not mean that there were no problems. Satan tried to destroy the unity. Luke has recorded that certain widows were being neglected in the daily distribution of food. This created unhappiness and complaints—in short, lack of unity. But the apostles, facing the problem with wisdom and discretion, appointed qualified men to handle the situation. The problem was soon solved. Once again unity was restored (see Acts 6:1-4).

What is more significant than these accounts of unity are the results of that unity. These appear again as a direct answer to Christ's High Priestly Prayer recorded in John 17. Jesus prayed that unity might reveal the fact that He had come in the flesh to save all people from their sins. In Acts 2, following Luke's report of unity in the Jerusalem church, we read that they enjoyed "the favor of all the people"—obviously the non-Christians in Jerusalem. We also read that "the Lord added to their number daily those who were being saved" (Acts 2:47).

As the church continued to grow, Luke later reported that "all the believers were one in heart and mind." Consequently, "The apostles continued to testify to the resurrection of the Lord Jesus, and much grace was upon them all" (Acts 4:32-33). Again, we see a direct correlation between unity in the body of Christ and the results of that unity in the lives of non-Christians.

It should not surprise us, then, that we see the same pattern in Acts 6, following the restoration of unity that was interrupted by the needy widows. Once they had faced the problem and solved it, "the Word of God spread. The number of disciples in Jerusalem increased rapidly, and a large number of priests became obedient to the faith" (Acts 6:7).

PRACTICAL STEPS FOR DEVELOPING UNITY IN YOUR CHURCH

Step 1

Realize first that unity is possible.

There is, of course, a spiritual unity that binds all believers together within the universal church. Even those we do not know—and never will know till we are in heaven—are one with us in Christ. But the unity that Jesus and Paul prayed for is a concrete, visible, and practical unity that can exist among believers who are bound together in a particular geographical location. It is day-by-day, gut-level unity. It involves flesh and blood people in relationship with each other. This is what was obvious in Jerusalem.

Unity and oneness are possible, then, in a local church. Though many different personalities are part of any given local family of believers, yet they can be drawn together as one heart and one soul.

This is a great mystery, but it is possible in Jesus Christ. If it was the spiritual dynamic in many of the New Testament churches (and it was, even where slaves and slave owners sat side-by-side as brothers in Christ), then it can also be true of the twenty-first-century churches who also "make every effort to keep the unity of the Spirit through the bond of peace" (Eph. 4:3).

Step 2

Realize that unity in a local church is not automatic.

As Paul exhorted, creating and maintaining unity takes effort. True—and as just stated—there is positional unity, because we are in Christ. But the practical and visible unity comes when every believer does his part.

Imagine what would have happened to the unity in the Jerusalem church if the apostles had not faced the reality of the neglected widows. No doubt it would have resulted in the first major local church split.

Imagine what would have happened if the leaders in Antioch had not faced the theological problem created by the Judaizers (Acts 15). If they hadn't solved the problem with the help of the Jerusalem council, it might have resulted in theological confusion and division all over the New Testament world. But because they faced the problem and did something about it, unity was restored.

All of this says that maintaining unity has two dimensions. First, Christ prayed (and is praying) for us. We have supernatural help available to defeat Satan. Second, we must "make every effort" to see that we do not allow human factors to create irritations to bring about misunderstandings that divide us. Satan delights in using trivia to destroy local churches.

Step 3

Realize that the key to unity is Christian maturity, reflecting love.

This, of course, is what the previous chapter is all about. And this is best illustrated (in a negative fashion) by the Corinthian church. They were woefully immature and unloving in their attitudes and actions. Consequently, they represent the most carnal, divisive, and disunified church in the whole New Testament world.

Step 4

Review the first three "one another" exhortations in chapters 1, 2, and 3.

When all believers function as "members of one another," when Christians are "devoted to one another in brotherly love," and when we all "honor one another above ourselves," we will be well on our way to being "of the same mind with one another." But, there's more, and the next chapter lays down another basic "one another" necessity if the church is to become a unified body.

DISCUSSION GUIDE FOR SMALL GROUPS

OPENING

Together brainstorm all the "units" that group members are part of (families, corporations, clubs, organizations, etc.). Then have each person answer: In which of these units do you feel the most sense of unity? How is that unity expressed?

FOR DISCUSSION

1. Do you agree that Satan's primary strategy involves destroying unity among Christians? Why would that be so effective? What examples have you seen of disunity within the church? What examples have you seen of Christians overcoming disunity?

2. Read John 17:20-25. If you had been one of the disciples who heard Jesus pray this prayer, how would you have reacted? What does it mean to you to know that Jesus prayed this prayer for you and the church of today?

3. How has God answered Jesus' request recorded in John 17:23? What roles do you think the two dimensions of supernatural assistance and human effort play in fulfilling this request of Jesus? How can we keep these two in balance?

4. Read Acts 2:42-47. What evidences of unity in the early church would you have found most compelling if you were an unbeliever

in that day? What evidences of unity do you see in your local church today?

5. In what areas does your church need to make a greater effort in demonstrating unity? Write them down. In which of these areas can you personally make a difference? How?

CLOSING

Reflect on the areas of disunity you listed. Remember the two dimensions of maintaining unity: divine assistance and human effort. As a group, pray for those group members who are in a position to make a difference in each area of disunity. Pray for God's help in restoring and maintaining unity in all the areas you listed.

For Next Time

1. Read chapter 5.
2. Continue to pray for unity and for those who need to take specific action to restore unity in specific areas.

Chapter Five

Accept One Another

Accept one another, then, just as Christ accepted you,
in order to bring praise to God.

Romans 15:7

I grew up in a church where "acceptance" by others depended primarily on what you did or did not do. As you might guess, the list of "dos and don'ts" did not comprise a biblical list. Rather, it consisted of extra-scriptural activities, most of which were cultural.

What I'm describing is legalism. Nothing shatters true spiritual unity among Christians more thoroughly than extrabiblical rules and regulations that we use to evaluate a person's relationship with Jesus Christ. When acceptance or rejection of others is based on a legalistic mind-set, it leads rapidly to judgmental behavior and pseudospirituality. It also creates false guilt, destroys personal freedom to really be what God wants a Christian to be, and often leads to a violation of the true biblical standards for Christian behavior. In fact, some Christians would never violate their cultural standards and yet violate very specific biblical responsibilities with every degree of regularity—such as not "accepting others" as Christ has accepted them.

A lot of wonderful people attended the church in which I grew up, and there was incredible loyalty within the group. Yet, there was little in-depth spirituality and lots of internal divisions. Those who became part of the group were accepted only as they fulfilled a predetermined set of behavioral expectations. Personally, I experienced false guilt for years—even after I left this religious community. It took a full five years for me to retune my conscience to the Bible rather than to the cultural standards I had been taught as a child. Even after I *knew* what was true spirituality in my head, my feelings still responded inappropriately.

This is a sad commentary on what Christianity has come to be in many situations. The Bible *does* lay down behavioral expectations for Christians, but it also condemns acceptance or rejection based on external patterns that go beyond specific scriptural statements.

LEGALISM VS. LICENSE

Before we move on to discuss what Paul really meant when he exhorted Christians to "accept one another," clearly understand that people often overreact to legalism and are caught in the "Peril of the Pendulum." They move from legalism to license—using their freedom in Christ to engage in activities that are unequivocally a violation of the will of God. They rationalize worldly behavior under the guise that they are "under grace"—not "under law."

Let's set the record straight. A true understanding of God's grace and the freedom that we have in Jesus Christ leads to holiness—not worldliness. Paul spelled this out clearly in his letter to Titus. It's a message that touched my life deeply and helped me understand God's plan for my life. Once we understand God's saving grace and when we truly appreciate what we have in Christ, how can we do less than respond to His love by offering our bodies back to Him as living sacrifices (Rom. 12:1-2)? Listen to Paul as he spelled out this great truth for Titus:

For the grace of God that brings salvation has appeared to

all men. It teaches us to say "No" to *ungodliness* and *worldly passions*, to live *self-controlled, upright* and *godly lives* in this present age, while we wait for the blessed hope—the glorious appearing of our great God and Savior, Jesus Christ, who gave himself for us to redeem us from all *wickedness* and to *purify* for himself a people that are his very own, *eager to do what is good* (Titus 2:11-14).

A KEY TO UNITY

In our last chapter, we looked at the concept of one-mindedness and why Jesus Christ and Paul prayed for this kind of unity. It's in this context that Paul exhorted believers to "accept one another." Note the context of the injunction:

May the God who gives endurance and encouragement give you a *spirit of unity* among yourselves as you follow Christ Jesus, so that with *one heart and mouth* you may glorify the God and Father of our Lord Jesus Christ. *Accept one another, then, just as Christ accepted you* (Rom. 15:5-7).

Paul used Jesus Christ as his example for acceptance. We are to accept other Christians just as Jesus Christ accepted us—which raises a very basic question. How did Jesus Christ actually receive us? Did He say, "I will accept you if you speak German"?—which incidentally, at one time, was a part of the division and disunity in the church in which I grew up. In fact, the whole church was permeated with German culture, which was often equated with biblical Christianity.

Obviously, Jesus does not accept us because we speak a certain language. Neither does Jesus accept us into His family based on our color, our status, our wealth, our age, or our sex. When we become Christians, Jesus Christ accepts each of us unconditionally. "It is by grace" we "have been saved, through faith." Salvation "is the gift of God" and we do not receive it "by works, so that no one can boast" (Eph. 2:8-9).

This truth is beautifully captured in the old hymn *Rock of Ages*:

Could my tears forever flow,
Could my zeal no languor know,
These for sin could not atone—
Thou must save, and Thou alone.
In my hand no price I bring,
Simply to Thy cross I cling.

Jesus Christ doesn't even ask us to clean up our act before He accepts us. Rather, He has said that He accepts us just as we are—our weaknesses and all. He tells us to come to Him and receive Him and He will clean up our act. This is what Paul meant after his great declaration that we're saved by grace through faith:

> For we are God's workmanship, created in Christ Jesus to do good works, which God prepared in advance for us to do (Eph. 2:10).

JUDGING ONE ANOTHER

To sit in judgment on other Christians is a violation of Paul's exhortation to "accept one another." Interestingly, the apostle used these two concepts concurrently to make his point in his Roman letter. He wrote: "Accept him whose faith is weak, without passing judgment on disputable matters" (Rom. 14:1).

In this particular New Testament church (and others like it), some Christians were refusing to engage in certain legitimate activities. These problems arose out of their previous sinful associations with those activities. Others, however, were free from this very real, but unwarranted, guilt.

In both the Roman and Corinthian churches, one of these activities involved eating meat that had been offered to idols. Paul, in his inimitable way, brought the problem into clear focus, particularly in his Corinthian letter:

> So then, about eating food sacrificed to idols: We know that an idol is nothing at all in the world, that there is no God

but one. . . . But not everyone knows this. Some people are still so accustomed to idols that when they eat such food, they think of it as having been sacrificed to an idol, and since their conscience is weak, it is defiled. But food does not bring us near to God; we are no worse if we do not eat, and no better if we do (1 Cor. 8:4, 7-8; see also Rom. 14:14).

How did Paul deal with this problem? First, he spoke to both the weak and the strong: "The man who eats everything must not look down on him who does not, and the man who does not eat everything must not condemn the man who does, for God has accepted him" (Rom. 14:3). In other words, we are not to judge each other in areas that are not specified by God as sin. "Each one," said Paul, "should be fully convinced in his own mind" (Rom. 14:5).

Second, after exhorting both mature and immature Christians not to judge one another, Paul then laid a heavy responsibility on mature Christians—those who could eat meat offered to idols without a guilty conscience:

All food is clean, but it is wrong for a man to eat anything that causes someone else to stumble. It is better not to eat meat or drink wine or to do anything else that will cause your brother to fall. . . . We who are strong ought to bear with the failings of the weak and not to please ourselves (Rom. 14:20-21; 15:1).

If we are truly mature, we will be sensitive toward our brothers and sisters in Christ who are not as strong as we are. We will be careful to do nothing that would cause them to stumble and fall into sin. If these two attitudes are working concurrently in a local body of believers, unity will inevitably emerge. Those who are weak will soon become strong, and those who are strong will become even more mature.

SHOWING PARTIALITY

Paul introduced showing partiality as a barrier to unity and acceptance of others in his letter to the Romans even before dealing with legalism. "Live in harmony with one another," he wrote. "Do not be proud, but be willing to associate with people of low position. Do not be conceited" (Rom. 12:16).

James called this sin "prejudice." He allowed no room for misinterpretation when he wrote, "As believers in our glorious Lord Jesus Christ, don't show favoritism" (James 2:1).

James was addressing a particular problem involving the rich and the poor. When a man came into their assembly well dressed and obviously rich, the leaders immediately gave him the best seat. But when a poor man came in, dressed in shabby clothes, they ushered him to a seat less prominent. When you do this, queried James, "Have you not discriminated among yourselves and become judges of evil thoughts?" (James 2:4). To make sure they really got his point, James spelled out the answer to his own questions in unequivocal terms: "If you show favoritism, you sin" (James 2:9).

SHOWING HONOR VS. SHOWING FAVORITISM

It's not wrong to honor others who are faithful to God with their material possessions—just as it is not wrong to honor Christians for being hospitable, sharing Christ with others, and serving the Lord in other ways. In fact, as we already noted in chapter 3, we are exhorted to actually "honor others." In terms of being generous, the apostles changed Joseph's name to "Barnabas (which means Son of Encouragement)" in order to honor him for using his material possessions to serve the church in Jerusalem (Acts 4:36-37). This is about as public as honor can get! But this is far different than showing "favoritism." All Christians should be honored in various ways for their faithfulness. In terms of generosity, it should be based on faithfulness in the light of what we have—not in terms of quantity.

Prejudice, favoritism, and discrimination in the body of Christ rejects and alienates some Christians and accepts others. This violates the laws of God. Furthermore, this kind of behavior violates the very nature of the functioning body of Christ. We are all one. Every member is important—rich or poor, young or old, black or white, weak or strong, Swedish or Norwegian, those who speak English and those who speak Spanish—or any other language. If we show favoritism, we also destroy the unity, harmony, and oneness in the body of Christ that Christ and Paul both prayed for and commanded.

BREAKING DOWN THE WALLS!

Tony Evans was one of my students at Dallas Theological Seminary. He was a young black man—one of the first on the Seminary campus at that time. I'll never forget Tony sharing with me what happened when he and his wife visited a well-known Bible-teaching church here in Dallas. Believe it or not, a deacon quietly but deliberately escorted this young couple to the door and told them they were not welcome in this church.

In spite of being potentially misinterpreted, I must share the sequel to this story. Tony went on to share with me that Fellowship Bible Church—the first church I founded here in Dallas—was the only white Bible-teaching church where he and his wife, Lois, felt welcome at that time. Later, they became our first full-time church planting team. The body at Fellowship Bible Church paid this couple's full salary for three years to help Tony carry out his own vision—to start a Bible-teaching church in the black community—a church now known around the world as Oak Cliff Bible Fellowship.

Tony's testimony was a real encouragement to me as a pastor since I'd already taught these "one another" concepts to my people. It was a thrill to see them practicing particularly the exhortation to accept others as Christ accepted them.

However, I share this story to also illustrate how much prejudice has existed in white churches that claim to believe and teach the Bible. True, our attitudes and actions have changed dramatically since the early 1970s, but may I also remind you that relatively speaking, this was not many years ago!

It is startling how some evangelical, Bible-believing churches over the years have justified prejudice. Of course, we can make the Bible teach anything we want—and this is exactly what we're doing when we bar any sincere and practicing Christian or non-Christian from attending a local church. When we do this, we are sinning against both God and man.

PRACTICAL STEPS FOR ACCEPTING ONE ANOTHER

Step 1

Make sure you really understand what Paul was teaching in Romans 14.

This passage is woefully misinterpreted and misapplied. First, Paul was teaching that neither the weak nor the strong are to judge one another. This is a two-way responsibility. In many twenty-first churches, the strong are expected to bear full responsibility. This, of course, is a violation of Paul's teaching.

Second, the strong Christian is to be careful not to cause a weaker brother or sister to fall into sin. Here is where many of today's Christians terribly misunderstand and violate Paul's teaching. "Offense" or "stumbling" is defined by some, especially immature Christians, as making them "feel bad" or uncomfortable. This is not what Paul meant by causing "distress" or "grief" or making someone stumble. Rather, he made it clear that accusing others of wrongdoing in this way is in itself judgmental. What Paul meant by "causing someone to stumble" is to cause a fellow Christian to actually sin against himself and the Lord.

Step 2

Evaluate your own attitudes and actions to see if you're accepting and rejecting others based upon your own standards that you have set up or accepted because of your own weak conscience.

Ironically, some Christians—when they are "weak" in their faith—actually set up extrabiblical standards for themselves. As time passes by and they become leaders of others, they then require that all Christians measure up to those same personal standards in order to be spiritual. Without knowing it, these people have allowed themselves to perpetuate their "weaknesses" and to judge those who are stronger than they are. This, of course, is also judging others and is not accepting others as we should.

I remember having to come to grips with this problem in my own Christian life. As a new Christian, certain types of musical styles—even with Christian words—troubled me, primarily because of my lifestyle before I became a Christian. I remember how disturbed I became when some Christians didn't have the same negative emotional reactions to this music as I did.

In retrospect, I now know I was being very judgmental. I simply assumed that because this music bothered me, it should bother everyone else. Unfortunately, I had set up a standard for myself and then generalized it as a mark of spirituality. In reality, I was the "weaker brother." Once I understood this, I was able to accept and appreciate various musical presentations. Furthermore, I realized I needed to educate my own conscience and retune it to the Word of God. Today I enjoy many different kinds of music—and even appreciate others who have tastes far different from my own.

What about sin? To accept others unconditionally doesn't mean accepting what the Bible clearly defines as sin. As we'll see in our next chapter, Paul immediately speaks to this issue. After exhorting Christians to "accept one another," he adds the other side of love—"admonishing one another." As we'll see, this in itself is a very important part of building up the body of Christ!

PERSONAL STANDARDS VS. INSTITUTIONAL STANDARDS

I personally believe that a Christian organization has the right to set up certain standards that are extrabiblical, and yet not violate the teaching of Scripture. However, the moment we begin to evaluate other Christians' spirituality on the basis of these standards, and begin to promote these standards as marks of Christian maturity, we violate the teachings of Scripture. We are using a false criterion for measuring spirituality.

However, having made allowance for institutional standards that are extrabiblical, may I present what I believe is a better way. If we teach and practice the true biblical criteria for spirituality, we will usually find it unnecessary to set up standards in addition to Scripture. Christians will learn to make decisions regarding their behavior based on true scriptural principles and precepts. When they do, they'll be operating from the heart rather than from the head. Their motivation will be internal rather than external. Furthermore, they'll learn to make decisions that are consistent and not hypocritical.

Step 3

Evaluate your attitude toward other Christians concerning prejudice and favoritism.

Prejudice is a very subtle sin. Do you realize it took the Apostle Peter at least five years after the Holy Spirit came at Pentecost to understand and accept the fact that Gentiles could be saved? Even then, it took a vision in which he saw a sheet lowered from heaven that was filled with all kinds of animals that were declared unclean in the Old Testament. A voice told him to "kill and eat." Peter refused, and the Lord told him not to "call anything impure" that He "has made clean."

At the same time, the Lord appeared to a Gentile named Cornelius who lived in Caesarea. He honored this man for his desire to do the will of God and told him to send for Peter—who reluctantly came and entered this Gentile's home and preached the Gospel (Acts 10:27-28). When the Holy Spirit came upon this entire household, it was then that Peter—the great leader of the apostles—understood for the first time that Jesus Christ died for the sins of all people. "I now realize," he said, "how true it is that God does not show favoritism but accepts men from every nation who fear him and do what is right" (10:34-35).

I can identify with this story. Since I was reared in a religious and cultural environment that taught me that we were somehow special in God's sight, I found it difficult to accept other Christians as being on the same level as we were—even though I knew in my head we were violating the will of God in many ways. Prejudice and pride cause us to overlook our sins. Ironically, it took me approximately five years as well to even recognize my prejudice—and only after I faced a serious crisis in my own faith. It took a very painful experience to show me what was really in my heart.

What about you? Can you truly accept all other believers as brothers and sisters in Christ? Is this actually happening in your church?

Step 4

Follow this three-point plan for overcoming any problem in your life that reflects legalism and prejudice:

1. Acknowledge it as sin (1 John 1:9).

2. Pinpoint the areas of your life where you need to change. Ask God to help you overcome your sins. Pray specifically about specific problems.

3. Take an action step. For a starter, select another member of Christ's body you have had difficulty accepting. Do something for that person that reflects true Christian love. For example, you might invite that person to your home for dinner.

Don't wait until you "feel" like changing or doing something about your sin. If you do, the feelings may never come. Christian love acts on what is the right thing to do.

If your church is permeated with legalistic behavior and/or prejudice, ask your pastor or some other leader in your church to read this chapter and to give you his opinion as to whether or not it is scriptural. If his reactions are negative, then graciously ask him to give you biblical reasons for his conclusions.

DISCUSSION GUIDE FOR SMALL GROUPS

OPENING

In the space below, make a sketch or paint a word picture of what acceptance looks like to you.

Explain your drawing or word picture to the rest of the group.

FOR DISCUSSION

1. What kinds of cultural standards for behavior (as opposed to biblical standards) have you observed in various churches or Christian communities? What extrabiblical standards does your own church have? How do those standards develop? How can they be helpful? How can they be harmful?

2. Read Romans 14:1–15:1. In what areas of behavior do you consider yourself a "stronger" brother or sister—one who feels comfortable with Christian liberty in those areas? How have others responded to your behavior in those areas? How have you responded to "weaker" brothers and sisters who are unsure that your behavior is right?

3. In what areas of behavior do you consider yourself a "weaker" brother or sister—one who feels uncomfortable with behavior that other Christians condone? How have you responded to those whose behavior differs from yours in those areas? How have they responded to you?

4. What issues cause you to struggle with whether certain standards are biblical or merely cultural? How can this group help you clarify your understanding?

5. What role do prejudice and favoritism play in your church? How can you work to promote acceptance instead?

CLOSING

Form pairs and have partners share their responses to Steps 2, 3, and 4 of "Practical Steps to Help Christians in Your Church Accept One Another." As partners, challenge each other, encourage each other, and pray for each other. Remember to maintain confidentiality!

For Next Time

1. Read chapter 6.
2. Continue to pray for your prayer partner.
3. Take the action step you identified in Step 4 of "Practical Steps to Help Christians in Your Church Accept One Another."

Chapter Six

Admonish One Another

And concerning you, my brethren, I myself also am convinced that you yourselves are full of goodness, filled with all knowledge, and able also to admonish one another.

Romans 15:14, NASB

Some of the most significant relationships I've developed over the years have resulted from experiences in which I've had to confront another Christian about sin. It has never been an easy task (I dread it every time). Yet in the end, it usually (not always) has been a very emotionally and spiritually rewarding task. Furthermore, it always provides me an opportunity for personal, psychological, and spiritual growth. I inevitably end up evaluating my own Christian lifestyle and frequently discover I need to make some changes too.

There is no greater sign of love than to be willing to risk rejection and broken relationships with others. And if admonishment is done in the right spirit, with the right motive, using an appropriate method, the person who is not living a life worthy of the Gospel of Christ usually senses the risk you're taking. Though that person may have difficulty acknowledging it at that moment, down deep he really knows. Someday he will probably thank you for your love.

WHY IS CONFRONTATION SO DIFFICULT?

I remember one very painful experience when I was in college and also serving in a Christian organization. I worked closely with a young man who had the reputation of irritating others on staff. He was always complaining and criticizing. When he began to spout off, others would simply roll their eyes and look the other way. But no one seemed to have the courage to confront him about his unbecoming behavior. They simply talked about him behind his back.

My relationship with this young man was particularly difficult. You see, we were roommates. Most of the time, I simply bit my tongue when I became exasperated. I didn't have the courage either to confront him—particularly because I didn't want to be rejected. That's the major reason why most of us don't admonish others when they are wrong.

Eventually, he decided to leave the organization. Most of us breathed a sigh of relief. But then one day shortly before he moved, I couldn't hold back my frustration and pent-up anger. Perhaps it was because I felt a sense of responsibility. Frankly, I'm not sure what my motives were—but I'll never forget the scene. We were eating together in a restaurant. Suddenly I poured out my negative feelings, sharing everything everybody was saying behind his back and interweaving my own intense frustrations. Having no choice, he simply sat and listened!

Then something happened. We got in the car to return to our apartment. I burst into tears! I must have wept for at least ten minutes. It was then that he began to soften and to respond with kindness. In retrospect, I think he actually enjoyed seeing me "out of control"—something he did all the time. In fact, people who have these problems will actually "push others" to see if they will lower their guard and behave like them. In a bizarre way, they actually *do* feel good when others demonstrate their own weaknesses.

I was surprised that he wasn't angry. Somehow, even though I blundered through my confrontation, he knew I loved him. He knew I was being vulnerable. You see, about two years later I received a letter from this young man thanking me for being honest. "I knew everything you said was true at the time," he said, "but I couldn't admit it then. I want you to know I have grown up!"

WHAT IS ADMONISHMENT?

Translators use various words to describe Paul's injunction to the Roman Christians. As we've seen, the *New American Standard Bible* reads "admonish one another." Williams uses the phrase *"counsel one another."* Beck, the word *"correct."* And the New International Version reads: "I myself am convinced, my brothers, that you yourselves are . . . competent to *instruct* one another."

The word *noutheteo* doesn't refer to casual communication or normal teaching and counseling. It implies a definite exhortation, a correction. In the Thessalonian letter, the translators of the *New International Version* have actually used the word "warn" to describe Paul's admonishment to Christians who were idle and lazy (1 Thes. 5:14).[1]

Paul's exhortation to "admonish one another" in this Letter to the Romans is a divine balance to his instructions to "accept one another." It may appear that we are to "accept" a person's sinful behavior. Not at all! We can "accept the sinner" without "accepting his sin." In fact, it's our unconditional acceptance of others that gives us the credibility to admonish and correct. By accepting others as Christ accepted us, we earn the right to admonish others who are straying from the straight and narrow path that God has outlined for us in Scripture.

One Sunday afternoon, I received a telephone call from a young man. He was angry—at me, the other elders in our church, and at the professors at Dallas Seminary. I was taken aback as I held the receiver to my ear, listening to him berate me and a number of other people—blaming all of us for his problems.

Fortunately, I had encountered this kind of "verbal attack" before. I am always caught off guard, but I was able to maintain my composure. I have learned that most people who take this kind of risk are actually crying out for help—even though their approach

---

[1]See also Acts 20:31 and 1 Corinthians 4:14. The NIV translators use the same

often alienates the very people they are crying out to. Strange as it may seem, they actually attack people they feel secure with—which is a "backhanded" compliment that is easily misunderstood—and understandably so!

In this case, my suspicions were right. This young man was crying out for help. Fortunately, I understood his motives, and even though I felt judged and angry feelings were beginning to well up within me, I didn't reject him—even though I felt like hanging up on him. Rather, I suggested that we meet the next day to talk about his feelings. At that moment, I sensed he was not in a mood to listen and I was definitely not in a mood to deal with his problem objectively. We both needed time to cool off.

When we met, he shared his real problems. You see, down deep he was angry at himself—and his employer. He lost his job and felt it was unfair. He was also angry at his wife because he didn't feel her total support (she probably knew down deep that he was at least partially responsible for what happened). What I heard was just as I had suspected. He had transferred his anger toward others to me and the other people he had mentioned the day before.

After this man had shared his deep hurt and pain at a more honest level, I told him that he would have made it much easier for me the day before if he hadn't attacked and blamed me for his predicament. If he had shared his hurt with "I feel" messages rather than with "you are responsible" messages, it would have been much less painful for both of us. In this less emotional context, I was able to interpret for him what had happened—how we all tend to blame others for our mistakes when we get ourselves into trouble.

I'll never forget this young man's response. He looked up at me with tears rolling down his cheeks. A rather sheepish grin appeared on his face as he said, "I know, but you are the first person who has ever loved me enough to tell me what's wrong with me!" At that moment, I knew I had communicated. The Holy Spirit had taken my words and penetrated his heart with some tough love!

I wish I could say that every situation turned out this way. Not everyone responds positively—even when we "speak the truth in love." And of course, there are times we don't handle these confrontations well ourselves. I could share experiences regarding other encounters where I now know I violated biblical principles, which in turn led to an unproductive result. This is why we need to look carefully at the biblical guidelines for engaging in this kind of communication.

WHAT MAKES US "COMPETENT TO ADMONISH OTHERS"?

Paul complimented these Roman Christians by letting them know he was thoroughly convinced that they were "competent to instruct [or admonish] one another." He spelled out why he felt this way.

1. They were *"full of goodness"* (Rom. 15:14a).

You are "competent," Paul said, because you "are full of goodness." Paul expressed his confidence in their basic spirituality, in their own progress in becoming like Jesus Christ. In other words, these believers were able to admonish one another because they were making progress in their own Christian lives. Though they weren't perfect, they were mature enough to make sure they had removed the "plank" from their own eyes before they tried to remove the "speck of sawdust" from a brother's eye (Matt. 7:3-5).

Christians who are sensitive about their own walk with God are capable—and responsible—to admonish other Christians. They have earned the right to warn those who display characteristics that violate the direct teaching of Scripture. Putting it another way, we must make sure we "clean up our own act" before we try to help others clean up theirs.

2. They were *"complete in knowledge"* (Rom. 15:14b).

The second requirement for being able to admonish others is an adequate knowledge of God's Word. Paul commended the Roman Christians for their maturity in this area.

Admonishment must be based on God's specific will and ways— *not on what we think* other Christians should or should not be doing. We must be careful at this point. Many Christians tend to confuse absolutes and nonabsolutes. If we exhort Christians in areas that are extrabiblical—areas that are not specifically spelled out in Scripture or specific things that involve cultural standards and practices—then we are in danger of imposing standards contrary to Scripture.

The difference sometimes represents a very fine line. A Christian engaging in an activity that is not specifically forbidden in Scripture may also be doing something that is definitely forbidden in Scripture. For example, the Bible does not specifically forbid reading modern literature or attending certain kinds of movies, but it certainly warns against exposing our minds to impure and unrighteous things (Phil. 4:8)—such as pornography.

Many of us have attended churches with a rather rigid list of do's and don'ts. These lists developed over time in response to cultural changes. Some had a definite scriptural basis. Others were simply activities which were put on the "no" list by church leaders because of their own spiritual struggles. It's important to realize that when we admonish other Christians, it should be based on scriptural lists of sins, not a list that we have added to the Bible. It's the scriptural list that carnal Christians respond to.

I have discovered this by experience. There is power and authority in the Word of God—even though some Christians will not make appropriate changes. I remember on one occasion admonishing a man who was attending our church on a regular basis. His wife, who also attended, had reported to me that her husband was sexually involved with another woman who attended another church. When I brought this charge to his attention in the most loving way I could, he didn't deny it. Furthermore, he knew that adultery was on God's "no list." However, he didn't agree to forsake the sin. Rather, he told me he knew he was out of the will of God. Furthermore, he informed me he didn't plan to change—but at the same time he reassured me he would not cause any problems in our church, either for me or his wife, by continuing to attend. He graciously removed himself. He wasn't angry at me—or the church. He simply decided to live out of the will of God. Even though he knew he would suffer the consequences, he understood very clearly the law of reaping and sowing.

ADDITIONAL BIBLICAL GUIDELINES

Fortunately the Bible gives us additional examples and exhortations that help us to carry out the process of admonishment.

1. Admonishment must be done with deep concern and love.

Paul exemplifies this principle in his own life. When he met with the Ephesian elders on his way to Jerusalem, he exhorted them to be on guard against false teachers. "Remember," he said, "that for three years I never stopped warning [admonishing] each of you night and day with tears" (Acts 20:31). There was no doubt in these men's minds that Paul loved them. Paul's tears were a reflection of his deep concern for these brothers in Christ. In no way could they interpret this process as being judgmental.

2. Admonishment must frequently be personal.

This does not mean that there should never be general admonishment. Paul did this when he wrote his letters to various churches. But Paul also reminded the Ephesian elders that he had warned *each of them*. And when he wrote to the Thessalonians, he stated:

> For you know that we dealt with each of you as a father deals with his own children, encouraging, comforting and urging you to live lives worthy of God, who calls you into His kingdom and glory (1 Thes. 2:11-12).

When a particular Christian has a problem, some pastors and teachers exhort the whole church, hoping the person who is in need of the exhortation is listening. This can simply be a way to avoid personal confrontation. Furthermore, the person on the listening end is smart enough to know what is happening and understandably resents it. In most instances, many others in the church also know who is being admonished from the pulpit—which only complicates the problem and adds to the offending party's anger and resentment. Far better to make such an exhortation a private matter. The results will be far more rewarding—even though you may be rejected.

Having said this, we also remember that the Bible does speak about "public rebuke," particularly for pastoral leaders, but only after personal confrontation and sufficient evidence of continual sin is given by two or three witnesses (Matt. 18:15-17; 1 Tim. 5:19).

3. Admonishment must be persistent if it is to be effective.

Note again that Paul's admonishment to the Ephesians was "night and day" and for a period of "three years." This kind of exhortation must be continual. It cannot stop after a brief encounter. The Word of God is filled with a multitude of exhortations, warnings, and instructions. It takes a lot of time to communicate them all—and a lifetime to apply them.

Personal confrontation and admonishment must also be persistent. We must realize, of course, that when a person rejects our admonishment and removes himself from the church, we have fulfilled our biblical responsibility—except to pray for that person. And if that individual eventually turns from sin and wants to return to the church, we should receive that person with open arms. This is practicing the exhortation to accept others as Christ has accepted us! If Jesus Christ forgives sin that is confessed, how can we not do the same thing?

4. Admonishment must flow from pure motives.

Again Paul serves as a great example. To the Corinthians he wrote: "I am not writing this to shame you, but to warn [admonish] you, as my dear children" (1 Cor. 4:14). We must do all we can to avoid embarrassing people—even those who are guilty. This is why personal confrontation should precede public confrontation. If an erring brother or sister is admonished privately and in Christian love, the need for public admonishment is often eliminated. Furthermore, if a person removes himself from the church, there is no need for public comment.

One church violated this biblical principle which actually led to a lawsuit. Let me say it again. Once a person leaves the church, there is no need for any further public communication—unless this individual continues to create confusion in the church. For example, the elders in our church had to confront a pastor who was living in an adulterous relationship. He left the church—after making a public confession—but then proceeded to lie and deceive a number of our people, giving the impression his sin was not as flagrant as it actually was. In this case, we wrote a letter to the church explaining what was really true. But before we sent it out, we met with this individual to verify once again the facts. In the presence of two witnesses, he acknowledged the truth. In this case, the problem was solved.

5. Admonishment must have the proper goal.

There should be only one basic objective when we admonish others: to help them become more mature in Jesus Christ. Thus Paul wrote to the Colossians: "We proclaim him, counseling [admonishing] and teaching *everyone* with all wisdom, so that *we may present everyone perfect in Christ*. To this end I labor, struggling with all his energy, which so powerfully works in me" (Col. 1:28-29).

6. Admonishment must be a natural outgrowth of proper body function.

There are two types of admonishment—preventive and corrective. The Scriptures teach us we are to warn each other to "stay away from sin" (preventive counseling). Though we have looked at this kind of communication, we have emphasized the corrective type. But preventive counseling should be consistent in the church as the body of Christ functions as a group. This is what Paul was referring to when he wrote to the Colossians:

> Let the Word of Christ dwell in you richly as you teach and counsel [admonish] one another with all wisdom, and as you sing psalms, hymns and spiritual songs with gratitude in your hearts to God (Col. 3:16).

PRACTICAL STEPS FOR APPLYING THIS PRINCIPLE TODAY
Step 1

Each of us must evaluate our own lives before trying to admonish others. The following questions will serve as personal criteria:

1. Can I say my own life is "full of goodness"?

2. Do I really know what the Bible teaches about godly and righteous living?

3. When I exhort or admonish another Christian (or Christians), do I do so reflecting deep love and concern?

4. When a Christian needs admonishment regarding specific sins, do I seek that person out in private, rather than use a public tactic that makes it appear I'm speaking to everyone?

5. Am I persistent in my admonishment without being obnoxious and overbearing?

6. Do I admonish others—not to tear them down and embarrass them—but to build them up?

7. Do I admonish others for one basic purpose—to help them become complete and mature in Christ?

Step 2

Evaluate your own church structures. Do they make it natural and easy for all members of Christ's body to be involved in "mutual admonishment"?

Many churches are not designed for proper body function. There is no opportunity for corporate sharing and "body life." Everything is so tightly programmed and structured that spontaneous instruction and counseling by members of the body cannot take place. If this is true in your church, you need to carefully evaluate your structures and make appropriate changes.

In our own church with several thousand people, we have designed the small group structure (which we call minichurches) for this kind of interaction to take place. In fact, it's in the context of these minichurches that we discover people who need admonishment. Furthermore, it is this context that establishes a climate of love, trust, and credibility. If the problem is unresolvable within this small group, it then creates a natural opportunity to refer the problem to the staff pastor assigned to oversee our small group ministry.

On one occasion, a divorced woman who had been a longtime member and was in one of our small groups, decided to live with a divorced man. The members of this group knew what had happened and attempted to deal with the problem. However, the woman resisted their efforts. They then came to me as senior pastor to help resolve the problem.

In this instance, I knew this woman well. In fact, we were good friends. Consequently, I simply made an appointment and went to the home where they were living together. We sat down at the kitchen table. In love, I admonished both of them. They sensed my love and my concern. Before the evening was over, they invited her son to join them in the kitchen. The man apologized to the boy and asked forgiveness. The woman—the boy's mother—also asked for forgiveness and told him to pack his bags because they were going to leave. "We don't belong here!" she said.

That night they separated after acknowledging their sin to God, seeking forgiveness from the Lord and from each other. However, the end of the story is very encouraging. Eventually, they decided to marry and live in God's will. I had the privilege of performing the wedding. Today, they are still very active members of our church and don't hesitate to tell this story to others.

The point is this. If it had not been for the small group structure, we may never have discovered the problem. Many people today can hide in our church structures. And when the sin is eventually discovered, it has often become a churchwide scandal—making it almost impossible to help the person repent. However, when you are in groups that are small enough, it is difficult to cover this kind of sin for very long. Even if a person suddenly disappears and no longer attends the group meetings, if relationships have been established, there will be follow-up—and eventually the truth will come out. This is what happened in this particular situation.

Step 3

If you are a parent (or planning to be one), reread the questions in Step 1.

How do you measure up as a parent or as a prospective parent? Are you indeed qualified to admonish your children? If not, remember you cannot suddenly become a "nonparent." Your only choice to be in the will of God is to become more qualified.

The same principle applies to every member of Christ's body. We cannot use our sense of being unqualified to exempt us from the responsibility to admonish one another. Rather, we are responsible before God to become mature in Christ so we in turn can help others become mature in Christ.

A WORD OF ENCOURAGEMENT

Remember that the Roman Christians were not perfect. There were definite problems in the church—as there are in every church today. Some people were weak, others were strong. Both the weak and the strong were judging one another. Otherwise, Paul would not have had to "admonish" them about this matter. But even with these weaknesses, Paul said:

> And concerning you, my brethren, I myself also am convinced that you yourselves are full of goodness, filled with all knowledge, and able also to admonish one another (Rom. 15:14, NASB).

Step 4

Use the words of the song "Lord Speak to Me" as a personal prayer.

> Lord, speak to me, that I may speak in living echoes of Thy tone;
> As Thou has sought, so let me seek Thy erring children lost and lone.
> O teach me, Lord, that I may teach the precious things Thou dost impart;
> And wing my words, that they may reach the hidden depth of many a heart.
> O fill me with Thy fullness, Lord, until my very heart o'erflow
> In kindling tho't and glowing word, Thy love to tell, Thy praise to show.
> O use me, Lord, use even me, just as Thou wilt, and when and where;
> Until Thy blessed face I see, Thy rest, Thy joy, Thy glory share.

DISCUSSION GUIDE FOR SMALL GROUPS

OPENING

Have each person complete the following sentences and share his or her responses with the group:

My attitude about receiving constructive criticism is . . .
> No pain, no gain.
> Grin and bear it.
> Ignorance is bliss.
> My attitude toward giving constructive criticism is . . .
> This is going to hurt me more than it hurts you.
> Let George do it!
> What goes around, comes around.

FOR DISCUSSION

1. Read Romans 15:14. What is the relationship between "admonishing one another" and "accepting one another"? (Rom. 15:7)

2. How would you define "admonishing one another"? Give some specific examples to illustrate your definition.

3. Based on Romans 15:14, how competent are the believers in your church to admonish one another? How competent are you? Why must we "earn the right" to admonish someone else? How willing are you to offer admonition? How willing are you to receive it?

4. Read Acts 20:31. What was the meaning of Paul's admonishing believers "in tears"? How can you keep your motivation pure? Why is personal admonition most effective? When should it move to involve the church as a whole?

5. Why is mutual admonition important to the body of believers? Is admonition in your church mainly preventive or mainly corrective? How has this small group been a form of "preventive admonishing" in your life?

CLOSING

Form pairs and have partners share their responses to Step 1 of "Practical Steps for Helping Christians to Properly Admonish One Another." As partners, challenge each other, encourage each other, and pray for each other. Remember to maintain confidentiality!

For Next Time

1. Read chapter 7.
2. Continue to pray for your prayer partner.
3. If you are a parent, work through the self-evaluation questions in Step 1 of "Practical Steps" as they apply to your relationship with your children. If possible, discuss them with your spouse—admonishing one another if necessary!

Chapter Seven

Greeting One Another

Greet Priscilla and Aquila. . . . Greet also the church that meets at their house. Greet my dear friend Epenetus. . . . Greet Mary, who worked very hard for you. . . . Greet one another with a holy kiss. All the churches of Christ send greetings.

Romans 16:3-6, 16

Several years ago, I walked into our church building one evening. A group of leaders and their families had gathered for fellowship. As I walked through the crowd that was assembling, I passed by a young high school student. "Hi, Bruce, how are you doing?" I said, as I went on to "greet" others. A few minutes later, one of our elders tapped me on the shoulder. "Gene," he said, "I have to admonish you for something."

At first, I thought Mike was kidding. He wasn't. "Gene," he continued, "you did something a moment ago that I often do myself." Incidentally, this is a very sensitive way to admonish a brother. He immediately disarmed me by sharing that he was at times guilty of the very thing he wanted to call to my attention.

When it dawned on me that Mike was serious, I responded immediately and asked what I had done. Mike proceeded to reconstruct the "Hi, Bruce, how are you doing?" scenario. "You asked him how he was doing," he said, "but you didn't stay around long enough to hear his response."

At that moment, Mike had my undivided attention! "What did he say?" I asked. Mike then proceeded to tell me that this young man had responded by saying— "I'm not very well. My brother was in a motorcycle accident today!"

Frankly, I was embarrassed, but thankfully Mike had the courage and concern to "tap me on the shoulder" and call this to my attention. I thanked him personally, found Bruce immediately, and apologized and asked his forgiveness for not listening to his response.

This experience taught me a great lesson. When we ask people how they're doing, we ought to stay around long enough to hear what they say. You see, it's so easy to become ritualistic in our "greetings"—to walk into church and ask, "How are you?" Often the responses are just as superficial—"Fine, thank you, and how are you?" We then move on to more brief encounters.

Don't misunderstand! Exchanging formalities is natural in every culture. Every time we say "hello" doesn't have to be a serious exchange. But frequently, we never get beyond the surface. In fact, at times we hope people won't really tell us how they're doing. We don't want to be bothered.

This experience also taught me another lesson. I'm so glad Mike took time to admonish me and to give me the opportunity to apologize. If he hadn't, I would never have known what I had done and I would not have become more sensitized to the importance of getting beyond the surface in our "greetings." This is why we need other members of the body of Christ.

A PERSONAL TOUCH

When Paul closed out his Roman letter, he extended a whole series of "greetings" to various people who meant a lot to him. He actually mentioned twenty-six people by name. Nothing means more to people than to be called by name—a social grace that takes much discipline, especially when we are meeting lots of new people all the time. Frankly, that's another area I need to grow in and give special attention.

After Paul mentioned these people by name and greeted them directly and indirectly with some very special words of commendation and appreciation, he closed out this series of special "hellos" by telling them to "greet one another with a holy kiss" (Rom. 16:16).

What did Paul mean? Does this injunction have any relevance for Christians today? Is this "one another" injunction purely cultural? We need to answer these questions—especially since this exhortation is repeated five times in the New Testament—four times by Paul and once by Peter (1 Cor. 16:20; 2 Cor. 13:12; 1 Thes. 5:26; 1 Peter 5:14).

ABSOLUTES AND NONABSOLUTES

In order to interpret scriptural exhortations properly, we must understand the difference between "absolutes" and "nonabsolutes." For example, we are to "teach and counsel one another." This is certainly a function. However, the Bible does not lock us into a particular form or structure for that process to take place.

We are also told to "preach the Word," but are not told specifically how. In these cases, teaching, preaching, and counseling are basic functions that take on various forms. In fact, it is impossible to have function without form. It is possible, however, to talk about a function without describing form or methodology. This the Bible does frequently.

Christians make a serious mistake when they superimpose particular cultural forms on biblical functions and then make the forms absolute as well as the functions. For example, some insist that preaching must always be from the pulpit, arranged with three points, and delivered with a forceful voice. The fact is, the Bible says nothing about the first two factors, and probably implies "loud voices" in most cases because they didn't have amplifiers.

Don't misunderstand. The Bible doesn't teach that these things are wrong. The Bible leaves us free to develop the forms that are most appropriate in any given culture, in order to carry out a normative biblical function.

Understanding the scriptural difference between function and form, supracultural absolutes and cultural nonabsolutes, helps solve many problems in biblical interpretation. With this in mind, the injunction to "greet one another with a holy kiss" also becomes an understandable concept—relevant in the twenty-first century as well as the first. On the one hand, the injunction, to "greet one another" is supracultural; on the other hand, the "kiss" represents a form of greeting very common in the first century. It is still common in some cultures today. We've all observed the heads of state in Middle Eastern and Eastern European countries greeting one another with a kiss. Most noticeable are the outward demonstrations by Russian leaders when they visit outside their country. They usually hold their host officials by both arms and then give a kiss on either the right or both cheeks. Understand, of course, that this greeting is often neither "holy" or "meaningful." It's pure protocol—just as Spanish-speaking people often say—"*Hola. ¿Cómo está usted?*" In turn, the other person responds—"*Bien, gracias, ¿y usted?*"

This is what I did when I met Bruce and in English asked—"Hello, how are you?" I expected him to respond—"Fine, how are you?" This was pure protocol. I never expected him to respond in any other way. This is why I missed his comment completely.

FUNCTION AND FORM

In some respects, this "one another" exhortation is different from the others. To this point, all of the injunctions we've looked at focus on function. However, to greet one another with a *holy kiss* includes both function and form. On the one hand, to "greet one another" is a function and normative. We are to do this in every cultural situation. The "form" of that greeting will vary. Put another way, as Christians, we're always to sincerely greet one another as brothers and sisters in Christ. However, the way that greeting is expressed depends on what is appropriate and expected in a given culture.

When I ministered among the Baptists in Russia and the Ukraine, I quickly discovered that they take this exhortation seriously and greet one another with a kiss on the lips—men with men and women with women. This was not totally surprising to me since this kind of greeting was practiced in the church where I grew up. I must admit that I was a bit taken back when a huge Belorussian—with whom I had developed a close relationship—put his arms around me as we were parting and planted three giant kisses on my lips. I find it relatively easy to adapt in various cultural situations—but in this instance, I'm fearful my culture shock was a little obvious.

Brazilian Christians have a different approach—at least in my experience. Men hug other men and men greet women with a kiss on each cheek—which must be initiated by the women. Single women, however, are greeted with a kiss, first on either cheek and then a third time on the first cheek.

I'll never forget the time my wife and I were ministering in New Zealand. We had the opportunity to attend a stage play that featured the ancient practices of the Polynesian people who first inhabited these beautiful islands. I was invited to the platform to participate in an ancient dance, which included physical greetings—namely, to "rub noses" with the other men on the platform. It was a rather awkward experience for me—but it taught me once again how customs and greetings vary from culture to culture.

In our culture, a handshake is very common and in more recent years, a hug. We have an older elder in our church—also a visitation pastor—who wears a button that says—"I Give Hugs." Hugging is his hallmark! And people love it.

Forms vary then from culture to culture. However, whatever forms these functions take in the Christian community, they should never violate biblical values. For example, in whatever way a "kiss" is expressed, it must always be "holy." This too is part of the supra-cultural dimension of this "one another" exhortation. Whatever we do, we must always reflect God's holy nature. As Peter wrote, we must "be holy" as God "is holy" (1 Peter 1:15).

THE "KISS" IN SCRIPTURE

The Bible gives several examples of greeting others with a kiss: Judas and Christ (Matt. 26:48-49); the father and his prodigal son (Luke 15:20); the Ephesian elders and Paul (Acts 20:37). Not one of these illustrations gives a specific description of the form the kiss took. Luke gives us a slight clue when he describes the parting scene between the Ephesian elders and Paul in Miletus. "And they all wept sore, and fell on Paul's neck, and kissed him"(Acts 20:37, KJV). Even here, the description is not very specific. We can only speculate from what we're told. It probably involved kissing his neck or his cheek. This, of course, conforms to the cultural practice of the day.

The ambiguity regarding "form" in Scripture is by unique design. Had the Holy Spirit specified a lot of form when He inspired the New Testament writers to describe New Testament functions, Christians all over the world would be attempting to copy form rather than function. Rather than allowing the biblical objectives to guide us in creating unique forms for a given moment in history and in particular cultures, we would lock ourselves into first-century patterns and structures. This is lethal to Christianity. The fact is, contemporary Christians are often guilty of making the Scriptures teach form when it is not even there. Think of what it would be like if there were an abundance of forms spelled out in the New Testament. The church would really be in trouble. We would lock ourselves into Middle Eastern culture.

SINCERE CHRISTIAN LOVE

Paul's and Peter's concern was not the form that the greeting should take, but that it be a "holy" one—a sanctified one—an expression of true Christian love. It was to demonstrate that believers were truly brothers and sisters in Christ. It was no longer to be just a greeting—a routine gesture that reflected the social graces of the particular culture. It was to be sincere and meaningful, reflecting God's care and concern for us all.

Greetings among people generally tend to be empty and superficial. As I illustrated from my own experience, people say, "Hello, how are you?" without any thought of wanting to know how you really are. Many people say, "It's been good to see you." Yet some couldn't care less if they ever see you again. Many people say, "I'm glad you came," while not caring if you'll ever come again. All of these, of course, are meaningless and empty, if not in many instances downright dishonest and hypocritical. Most of us, however, make these comments out of pure cultural habit.

Paul's concern (and Peter's) was that these New Testament Christians would greet one another with pure motives. Each greeting was to be a true expression of concern and love. When Christians greet one another today, the greeting must reflect the same dynamic. There is no place for hypocrisy and dishonesty among members of Christ's body.

OVERCOMING CULTURAL BARRIERS

There are times when our cultural background keeps us from practicing biblical directives. For example, my wife, Elaine, was reared in a home where physical affection was almost nonexistent. My experience was just the opposite. Even today, I still kiss my mom who is still living as well as my adult brothers and sisters.

When I became engaged, I felt it was only appropriate to do the same with Elaine's mother. However, when I tried to kiss her on the cheek, she instinctively withdrew, reflecting what she had learned in her particular culture. However, understanding these emotional barriers, I was not to be deterred. The next time I met her, I greeted her with a kiss—but this time, with less resistance. Eventually, she met me halfway across the room, actually initiating the greeting. In fact, the time came that if I didn't kiss her when I met her, I was in serious trouble. You see, down deep she wanted that kind of experience all along. However, the culture had restricted her all those years.

In this case, my mother-in-law's culture was out of harmony with biblical teachings. And when this happens, "culture" has to move over and make room for Christians to practice biblical truth. This happened all the time in the New Testament world.

PRACTICAL STEPS FOR APPLYING THIS PRINCIPLE TODAY
Step 1

Make sure you are living in harmony with other brothers and sisters in Christ.

You cannot greet others sincerely if you do not really care about them, or if there is something between you and another Christian brother or sister. The first step in getting back into God's will is to correct that problem. If you have been sinned against, go to that person and share why you feel the way you do. On the other hand, if you have sinned against someone else, immediately take the initiative and ask forgiveness.

In this kind of interchange, be prepared to discover that you may be as wrong as the other person, though you feel it's all his fault. Bad feelings often exist among Christians today because of misunderstandings and a breakdown in communication. Each sincerely feels the other person is wrong.

I'm reminded of the little boy who one day was walking along the railroad tracks with his father. "Look, Dad," the boy said, "the railroad tracks come together down there." "No, son," the father replied. "They never come together. It just looks that way."

Later, after the boy returned home, he told his mother that his daddy had lied to him. "Daddy told me the railroad tracks never come together," the boy reported, "but I know they do. I saw them."

How many Christians accuse others of telling untruths when it's a matter of limited perspective. What appears to be "tracks coming together" continue to be "parallel." We just don't see the whole picture.

Step 2

Make every effort to develop sincere interest in others.

If we are not sincerely interested in other people's interests, we will never feel comfortable greeting them. We will always be avoiding them or even running away—often blaming other people for not being interested in us.

If you have difficulty expressing sincere affection and love for other Christians, your problem may be rooted in one of two sources. Either you are a self-centered person because you always think of yourself first and have built the world around yourself. Or perhaps you feel uncomfortable with people because you are fearful and have deep feelings of inferiority.

There is only one basic solution to both of these problems—no matter what the root cause. You must forget about yourself. You must reach out to others. With God's help, you can! And though it may be painful—especially if your problem is psychological—you must begin to experience the benefits of relational Christianity. If you don't, you will never grow spiritually as you should. Furthermore, you will not be functioning fully as part of the body, helping other people to grow.

Step 3

Consider the aspects of physical affection in greeting other Christians.

First-century Christians greeted one another with more than words. This is a certainty. A kiss—no matter how it is expressed— involved physical contact with the other person. It probably involved both sexes. Could it be that Christians have been so concerned with the "dangers" of touching that we have gone to the other extreme?

There are dangers, of course, when Christians generally show physical affection to each other, particularly toward the opposite sex. If people are vulnerable to sensuous behavior, they will probably engage in inappropriate thoughts and actions no matter what the situation. But, there can also be dangers in "just talking" to Christians of the opposite sex.

Following are several guidelines that will help Christians avoid problems in showing physical affection—particularly to those of the opposite sex.

1. Men and women who are not related should always be discreet about showing physical affection.

2. Intimate physical affection between unmarried people should rarely be expressed in private situations. Even people who are seriously looking forward to marriage should guard themselves at all times.

3. Pastors and professional counselors must be especially cautious about showing physical affection—particularly in private. An emotionally or spiritually sick person can destroy another's reputation through gossip. Such a person might exaggerate any show of affection because of vain imagination.

Furthermore, we cannot ignore the current trend toward accusing people of sexual harassment. This has become a plague in our society. In fact, people are often set up by another person, just to form the basis for a lawsuit. As Christian leaders particularly, we must be extremely cautious—without ignoring the importance of "the healing touch."

4. Unmarried Christians should never show physical affection in such a way so as to stimulate the sensuous nature of the other person, causing improper thoughts and actions.

5. Some people who are more vulnerable to sin must always be more cautious than others in showing physical affection to the opposite sex.

I talked with a young woman once who complained that her father who is a Christian insisted on sensuously kissing her on the lips. I later discovered that this man had a very unsatisfying relationship with his wife. Obviously, he was vulnerable sexually, even in expressing affection to his own daughter.

A FINAL WORD

Mature Christians can and should show physical affection. In our society, shaking hands, a kiss on the cheek, and a gentle, nonsensuous embrace are certainly appropriate. Most Christians can express this kind of affection. But it must always be based on pure motives, discretion, and above all, true Christian love. When it is expressed in this manner, it can create oneness, unity, and even spiritual and psychological healing. But when it is expressed inappropriately, reflecting impure motives, indiscretion, and selfish actions, it can lead to hurt, bitterness, and even immorality. But isn't this true of almost every ingredient in Christian relationships?

DISCUSSION GUIDE FOR SMALL GROUPS

OPENING (Choose One)

1. Before the group meeting, arrange to have several group members dress up and greet other members according to the custom of different cultures. Here are some possibilities:

> Russian: Dress in a Russian cap and fur-trimmed coat. Greet arrivals with a bear hug and a kiss on the right cheek.
> Eskimo: Dress in a hooded parka. Greet arrivals by holding both their arms below the shoulders and rubbing noses.
> Asian: Dress in Asian clothing. Greet arrivals with a bow.
> Corporate: Dress in a business suit. Greet arrivals with a brisk handshake.

2. Form teams of three. Have each team list what they consider to be the top five insincere or cliché greetings. Compare lists, awarding each team a point for every time one of their statements appears on another team's list. Discuss: If you used one of these greetings only when you really meant it, how often would you say it? What purpose do these greetings serve if we really don't mean what we're saying?

FOR DISCUSSION

1. What is the distinction between a normative biblical function and a non-normative cultural form? What is normative in the injunction to "greet one another with a holy kiss"? What is cultural? If Paul were writing the same command to Christians today, how might he word it?

2. What significance does the function of greeting have among a group of Christians? Why do you think it is important enough to merit mention five times in the New Testament?

3. Read Colossians 3:12-14. How can Christians reflect this kind of relationship in our greetings? What forms might those greetings appropriately take?

4. What level of physical contact do you consider appropriate among Christians when they are greeting one another? In what situations would you consider more physical contact appropriate? How can you safeguard against abuse? Against being misunderstood?

5. Do you have any cultural barriers that cause you to violate the biblical exhortation to "greet one another with a holy kiss"?

CLOSING

Develop a group greeting that you can use when you see other group members. For example, you might like to combine a statement that each member of the group finds meaningful (something like "God be with you") with a gesture or embrace. Whatever you choose, talk through its significance so that it becomes a meaningful ritual for your group, not merely another cliché greeting. Use your greeting to close the meeting after praying together.

For Next Time

1. Read chapter 8.
2. Think and pray about ways to greet other Christians in a way that is both culturally acceptable and biblically right.
3. If you are single and in a dating relationship, discuss the guidelines in this chapter for maintaining purity.

Chapter Eight

Serve One Another

> You, my brothers, were called to be free. But do not
> use your freedom to indulge the sinful nature; rather,
> serve one another in love.
>
> *Galatians 5:13*

A budding artist once painted a picture of the Last Supper. He took
it to the writer, Leo Tolstoy for his opinion. Carefully and under-
standingly, the Russian master of words studied the canvas. Then
pointing to the central figure, he declared; "You do not love Him."

"Why, that is the Lord Jesus Christ," exclaimed the artist.

"I know," insisted Tolstoy, "but you do not love Him. If you loved
Him more, you would paint Him better."

Few of us are budding artists in this sense, but the Bible
teaches we're all to be *servants*—servants of the Lord Jesus
Christ and of one another. With this in mind, we can easily
reword Tolstoy's statement to read, "If you loved Him more, you
would serve Him better." Furthermore, "If we *loved one another
more*, we would *serve one another better*." As Paul wrote to the
Galatians, "You, my brothers, were called to be free. But do not
use your freedom to indulge the sinful nature; rather, *serve one
another in love*" (Gal. 5:13).

WE ARE TO BE SERVANTS

There are four basic words in the language of the New Testament that are often translated "serve," "servant," or "serving." All in all, this basic concept is used over 300 times (about 130 times in the Gospels and Acts and approximately 170 in the Epistles).

The two words that are used more frequently are *douleo* and *diakoneo*. *Douleo* literally means to be a slave, to serve, to obey, to submit. It's used in both a good and bad sense. On the positive side, the word means to serve God and others in a context of Christian love. On the negative side, *douleo* means to become a slave to some base power. For example, in Paul's Letter to the Romans he taught that people can be "slaves to sin" (Rom. 6:6).

Diakoneo means to "minister" to someone. In a more specific sense, New Testament writers used this word to describe someone who serves people food and drinks, someone who cares for others' material needs. In a more general sense, it describes those who attend to *anything* that may serve another's interest. It is from this concept that we get the word "deacon."

It's clear from these definitions that the first word, *douleo*, is the stronger in meaning. Some form of the word is used approximately 160 times in the New Testament. A *doulos* was a slave, a bondman, a person who served. In its strongest sense, this word describes someone who has given himself up completely to another's will. And this is the concept that Paul used when he wrote, "serve [*douleuo*] one another in love" (Gal. 5:13). He was writing about serving one another in the most devoted sense. As believers, we are to give ourselves totally to one another—to literally become slaves to one another.

What a contrast to the emphasis in modern society! Look at the newsstands and survey the titles of current magazines with their focus on "me" and "myself." The thrust of these publications are that I am important; my rights are what are the most significant thing. If my rights conflict with your rights, I come first. If you cannot meet my needs and I cannot meet your needs—if we can't work it out together—you go your way and I'll go mine.

In his book *Improving Your Serve*, Chuck Swindoll identified this emphasis with a verbal pyramid. At the top is "I," moving down to "me," "mine," and "myself."

I

ME

MINE

MYSELF

Why do people function this way? The Bible answers this question. It reflects the sin principle that is active in us all. Ever since Adam and Eve disobeyed God, all of us have become self-oriented. Men have become dominant and often cruel, not only in their attitudes and actions toward women, but toward all other human beings. Women have often become selfish, unsubmissive, and resistant to any form of authority. True, much of this is a reaction against male dominance and selfishness, but in its roots it is also a reflection of sin that infected the whole human race. Left to ourselves, we concentrate on ourselves—our rights, our needs, our interests. This is our natural bent.

How can we be set free from this problem? Paul answers that question.

WE ARE TO SERVE ONE ANOTHER

Jesus Christ made it possible for all of us to break out of our self-oriented mold. In Christ, we are set free to minister to others, to love others as ourselves (Gal. 5:14). When we become Christians, we are given new life—eternal life—and with that great gift we are given the potential and the power to get beyond ourselves and experience the fulfillment that comes to those who serve others. This is what Jesus Christ meant when He said, "For whoever wants to save his life will lose it, but whoever loses his life for me will find it" (Matt. 16:25).

Christianity is relational. First, it involves a personal relationship with Jesus Christ. We become Christians, not just by acknowledging that the Lord Jesus Christ is the Son of God, but by receiving Him as our personal Savior. John wrote that "to all who received him, to those who believed in his name, he gave the right to become children of God" (John 1:12). And when we receive Jesus Christ in this sense, we have a unique relationship with Him.

But a new relationship to Christ and with Christ is more than *vertical*. It is also *horizontal*. We become members of Christ's body, the church. By one Spirit we are all placed into one body (1 Cor. 12:13).

As we saw in chapter 1, we are "members of one another." Just as there are many interrelated and coordinated members in a human body, so it is within Christ's body. Each of us is related to all other parts of that body (v. 26).

WE ARE TO SERVE ONE ANOTHER IN LOVE

Serving one another must be guided by true love. Paul told the Galatian Christians they were "called to be free." However, they were not to use that "freedom to indulge the sinful nature" (Gal. 5:13a). In other words, it is possible to serve others in an inappropriate and carnal way.

What should guide us in our relationships with others? We are, Paul wrote, to "serve one another *in love*." To make the point even clearer, he reminded the Galatians that "the entire law is summed up in a single command: *'Love your neighbor as yourself'*" (v. 14).

The two basic words for love used in the New Testament (*agapao* and *phileo*) are used over three hundred times. Almost exactly half the times, this concept is used to refer to our relationship with God and the other half to our relationship with one another. This is very significant in view of Christ's answer to the Pharisees when they asked, "Which is the greatest commandment?" Jesus answered: "*Love the Lord your God* with all your heart and with all your soul and with all your mind.' This is the first and greatest commandment. And the second is like it: *'Love your neighbor as yourself.'* All the Law and the Prophets hang on these two commandments" (Matt. 22:36-40).

Other New Testament writers verify that love is the divine principle that should guide us in our relationships. John, particularly, emphasized this point. In his first epistle, he used the word love nearly fifty times. Five times he expressly wrote, "Love one another" (1 John 3:11, 23; 4:7, 11-12).

The Apostle Paul again and again demonstrated in his letters that love is the most important criteria in measuring the quality of Christian relationships. Note the following statements:

> And now these three remain: faith, hope and love. But the greatest of these is love (1 Cor. 13:13)
> Follow the way of love (14:1)
> Do everything in love (16:14)
> Be patient, bearing with one another in love (Eph. 4:2)
> [Speak] the truth in love (4:15)
> Live a life of love, just as Christ loved us and gave himself up for us (5:2)
> And over all these virtues put on love (Col. 3:14)
> Pursue . . . love (2 Tim. 2:22)

Love, as it is defined in Scripture, is the guiding principle in all Christian relationships, including the process of serving one another. Without Christlike love, our relationships will be dominated by selfishness and painful bondage. Serving others becomes a negative experience rather than a positive one. But guided by the divine principle of love, serving others becomes a powerful illustration of corporate Christlikeness.

FREEDOM TO SERVE

I never cease to be amazed when I board a huge jumbo jet. I experience firsthand the law of aerodynamics at work. For example, the huge Boeing 747 seats up to 500 passengers and when fully loaded with people, luggage, and fuel, it weighs up to 400 tons.

When ready for takeoff, the crew activates four huge jet engines. The thrust is so powerful you can actually feel yourself pushed back against your seat. Less than a minute later, that huge machine that measures nearly the distance of a football field is airborne, climbing skyward to a normal altitude of nearly 40,000 feet and traveling nearly 600 miles an hour.

People who travel a great deal take this experience for granted, but can you imagine what Orville and Wilbur Wright would have thought and felt if they could have been part of this incredible phenomenon. They would probably have been candidates for a cardiac arrest!

What is so amazing is that the law of gravity dictates that something so huge and so heavy should never get off the ground. In fact, I am six feet tall and weigh about 190 pounds. Yet, I have never been able to jump high enough to dunk a basketball in a ten foot hoop. To be able to do so, I would have to overcome the law of gravity.

This helps explains why a 747 weighing so much can lift off the runway and soar like an eagle. Its powerful jet engines and engineering design defy the law of gravity. In this instance, the law of aerodynamics at work through human ingenuity is more powerful than the law of gravity.

This principle is also true in the spiritual realm. The "law of sin and death" is active in every human being who has ever lived (Rom. 8:2). But the Scriptures also reveal a law that is greater and more powerful and which can be activated, not by human engineering, but by God Himself. It is the "law of the spirit of life" that was made available by the coming of Jesus Christ (v. 2). It is this law that sets us free to serve God and others in love. This is why Paul discusses serving in the context of freedom. If we are not "free in Christ," we cannot be "free to serve" as God intended. Paul wrote, "You, my brothers, were called to be *free*. But do not use your *freedom* to indulge the sinful nature; rather, serve one another in love" (Gal. 5:13).

FREEDOM IN CHRIST: AVAILABLE THROUGH FAITH

Paul began this section in his Galatian letter with a statement on freedom. However, he had already introduced this concept when he wrote, "It is for *freedom* that Christ has set us free" (5:1).

To understand this wonderful spiritual reality more fully, we must look at another letter Paul wrote, his Epistle to the Romans. After culminating a very intriguing section of Scripture dealing with the conflict that often exists between a Christian's old and new natures, Paul concluded—

Therefore, there is now no condemnation for those who are in Christ Jesus, because through Christ Jesus the law of the Spirit of life set me free from the law of sin and death (Rom. 8:1-2).

Jesus Christ is our source of freedom. And the Scriptures make it clear that the freedom in Christ is available through faith. Thus Paul wrote:

Therefore, since we have been justified through faith, we have peace with God through our Lord Jesus Christ, through whom we have gained access by faith into this grace in which we now stand (Rom. 5:1-2).

FREEDOM IN CHRIST: APPROPRIATED BY ACCEPTANCE

When is a Christian free? The Bible teaches that as believers we "have been set free from sin" the moment we truly put our faith in Christ (Rom. 6:18, 22). When we become Christians, sin is no longer our master (v. 14). When by faith we trust the Lord Jesus Christ as our Savior, we identify with His death. In the process, we actually die with Christ. Paul wrote that "our old self [old nature] was crucified with him so that the body of sin might be done away with, that we should no longer be *slaves* to sin" (v. 6). Paul states further that "anyone who has died has been *freed* from sin" (v. 7).

Don't misunderstand. Nowhere does the Bible teach that we are "free from sin" in the sense that we will no longer be tempted to sin, or that we will never sin, or that we do not have freedom to sin. That is why Paul warned the Galatians not to use their freedom in Christ "to indulge the sinful nature" (Gal. 5:13). What the Bible *is* teaching is that we are free from the *power* of sin. We don't have to serve sin and the old nature. The prison door is open. All we have to do is walk out into a new world.

When Corrie ten Boom was given notice that she was going to be released from a Nazi prison camp, she was led to the courtyard and from there to the prison gates. Later she wrote:

The gate swung open and I glimpsed the lake in front of the camp. I could smell freedom.

"Follow me," a young girl in an officer's uniform said to me. I walked slowly through the gate, never looking back. Behind me I heard the hinges squeak as the gate swung shut. I was free, and flooding through my mind were the words of Jesus to the church at Philadelphia: "Behold, I have set before thee an open door, and no man can shut it" (Rev. 3:8, KJV).

If Corrie had not accepted the fact that she was free and had returned to her dormitory rather than walking through the gate, she would have chosen to stay in prison rather than accept her freedom. Theoretically she would have still been free, but not experientially.

And so it is with many Christians. The prison door is open and we have been set free. Sin is no longer our master. But unfortunately, many Christians don't walk through the prison door and out into the sunlight of God's grace and love. We choose to stay in the wrong environment, the wrong place, and associate with the wrong people. We do not appropriate our freedom—which leads to the next step to freedom.

FREEDOM IN CHRIST: ACTIVATED BY OBEDIENCE

The crew in a 747 could sit at the end of the runway all day long, *knowing* that the plane is *free* to take off. They may have received clearance from the tower again and again. They also know that the power is available. But the plane will never get off the ground unless the jet engines are activated. The plane must be in a moving position.

Just so with a Christian. I can *know* I am free in Christ. And I can *accept* that truth as a reality. But I will never live above this world's system without obeying God's Word. It is the truth *applied* that really sets me free.

Nothing can compare with the freedom we experience when we walk in harmony with the Creator of the universe, conforming our lives to His will and desires. This does not mean we lose our individual personalities in some corporate entity. Neither does it mean we lose our self-identity. Rather, we are free to become all that God created us to become. We are set free from ourselves—free to reach out, to give, to share—in short, we are free to serve God and one another. We truly lose our lives to find them again.

SERVANTS OF RIGHTEOUSNESS

One day I was reading the *Dallas Morning News* and saw an article entitled "Of Manners, Respect and Consideration for Others." It was written by Bob St. Johns. He was sitting in a restaurant with a friend. He noticed what he described as a "big, chubby guy" sitting at a table with a young lady. "The big, chubby guy just sat there smiling, glassy eyed," Bob observed. "One time, he seemed to be cranking up to say something but, apparently, the moment passed or the light bulb went out in his head."

Continuing, Bob reported that the "guy just kept reaching out and hugging" the young lady. "She just leaned against him, looking blank."

"'Hey,' he finally said. 'You ready? Let's go,' and he smiled as if he knew a secret. He got up and started walking out."

"The young lady got up and followed the guy through the door. But about thirty minutes later the young lady reappeared—*without* her chubby friend. Asked what happened, she reported, 'We went in separate cars. He was following me to my apartment, but I made a quick turn and managed to lose him. He's a creep anyway.'

"A few minutes later, however, the 'big, chubby guy' also reappeared on the scene. '"Oh, hi,' said the young lady. 'What happened to you? I was worried.'"

When I read this story, I couldn't help but think of Paul's exhortation to the Galatians to "serve one another." It illustrates that all of life is relational. Either we are going to serve one another in love, or we're going to take advantage of one another since we all have social needs. On the one hand, this woman didn't like the guy. She probably knew he was going to use her for selfish reasons. She had been down that road before. On the other hand, from an emotional perspective, she probably needed another human being in her life. She wanted a relationship, superficial though it might be. On this particular evening, she somehow convinced herself she could do better. But when all was said and done, she couldn't escape from her relational needs.

LIFE IS RELATIONAL

As people, we are part of a human family. Whether a woman lives in a "playboy" mansion or in a convent; whether she is a wife or a mistress—she is obligated to and dependent on someone else—at least one other person and usually more. Whether a man is a corporate executive or pastor; whether he is President of the United States or the leader of the local drug ring—he *must relate* to others. It is impossible to live apart from some kind of human relationship that has certain reciprocal responsibilities. We do not—and we cannot—live in isolation from one another. We are dependent on each other to meet one another's needs—physically, emotionally, socially—and yes, spiritually.

This is by design—God's design. It has been true from the beginning of time. When God created Adam, He said, "It is not good for the man to be alone. I will make a helper suitable for him" (Gen. 2:18). Consequently, God created a woman for Adam. This began the human family and its responsibilities.

As believers in Jesus Christ, we are part of a unique family—the family of God. Not only is it a family with human dimensions, but also with divine dimensions. And when Paul exhorted the Galatian Christians to "serve one another in love" (5:13), he was well aware of the relational realities of life, both in the human family as well as in the Christian family. Thus, before he issued this "serving" directive, he wrote, "Do not use your freedom to indulge the sinful nature" (v. 13).

ACTS OF THE SINFUL NATURE

When Paul wrote to the Galatians, he stated that "the acts of the sinful nature are obvious" (5:19). Sin permeated their lifestyle before they became believers. They knew the acts of a sinful nature. But just to set the record clear for the Galatians—and for Christians of all time—Paul listed them (vv. 19-21):

Sexual Immorality	Fits of Rage
Impurity	Selfish Ambition

Debauchery	Dissensions
Idolatry	Factions
Witchcraft	Envy
Hatred	Drunkenness
Discord	Orgies
Jealousy	

"I warn you," Paul continued, "as I did before, that those who live like this will not inherit the kingdom of God" (v. 21).

Does Paul mean by this final statement that a person who "indulges his sinful nature" in any of these areas cannot be a Christian? The answer is a decided no. Rather, Paul is saying that this is the lifestyle of those who do not know Christ. But in this passage in Galatians, he is also saying that a true Christian *will be tempted* to "gratify the desires of the sinful nature" (v. 16). That will always be a reality until we are with Christ in heaven. However, he is also saying by implication that a true believer who loves Christ and others will not continue to be a "slave to sin" and to the "old nature." A true believer will become in actuality a "slave to righteousness." He will use his freedom to serve others in love rather than to serve others selfishly and in fleshly and carnal ways.

THE FRUIT OF THE SPIRIT

How do we recognize Christians who "live by the Spirit"? They will manifest the fruit of the Spirit in their relationships with others. Paul outlined these qualities next (Gal. 5:22-23). In his prayer for the Philippians, he identifies these qualities as the "fruit of righteousness" (Phil. 1:11):

Love	Goodness
Joy	Faithfulness
Peace	Gentleness
Patience	Self-control
Kindness	

These qualities are in stark contrast to the "acts of the old nature." So Paul concludes, "Since we *live by the Spirit,* let us *keep in step* with the Spirit. Let us not become conceited, provoking and envying each other" (Gal. 5:25-26).

A "BIRD'S-EYE VIEW"

It's important at this point that we get the big picture regarding Paul's emphasis on this passage. Paul's main concern is that we "serve one another in love" rather than "serving one another in carnal, fleshly ways." If we follow the old nature, our relationships with others will very quickly become immoral, impure, and idolatrous. Relationships will reflect hatred, discord, jealousy and fits of rage, selfish ambition, dissensions, and factions. No one would deny that all of these concepts are relational in nature, but they are oriented toward ourselves.

By contrast, if we "serve one another in love," we will meet one another's needs in unselfish ways. The results will be *more love* among us. People will be *joyful and happy.* There will be a sense of *peace, tranquility,* and *unity.* We will treat one another with *patience* and *kindness.* We will do what is *right* in our relationships. We will be *faithful* to one another according to the guidelines of Scripture. We will treat each other with *gentleness* and exercise *self-control* so that we don't use people for our own selfish ends.

If we live in the Spirit, we will reflect the fruit of the Spirit and our relationships will be characterized by *righteousness.* Thus, to be a servant to others in love, we must first of all be servants of righteousness. It is our commitment to following the leadership of God's Holy Spirit that keeps "serving others" from becoming a relational trap.

WHAT ABOUT YOU?

How are you relating to others? Your needs are important, but are you using others selfishly? Are you indulging your old nature? Are you allowing others to serve you without your serving them? Are you simply a receiver and not a giver? Or, are you following God's Holy Spirit? You can check yourself. Paul's two lists will help you be very specific. Check those areas that characterize your relationship with others. If you are honest, you will soon determine if you are a servant of righteousness or a servant of unrighteousness in your dealings with others.

PRACTICAL STEPS FOR SERVING ONE ANOTHER IN LOVE
Step 1

Evaluate how much you and others in your church may be reflecting "the acts of the sinful nature" in your relationships rather than "the fruit of the Spirit."

One way to get at this information is to begin with the following questions. The answers give indication of Christian maturity in a body of believers. A seven-point scale is included to help you measure various manifestations of Christlikeness. The number 1 signifies that the particular characteristic being evaluated is never visible. The number 7 indicates it is always visible. The numbers in between represent degrees of visibility.

	Never visible				Always visible		
1. Is there Christian love being expressed among one another in my church?	1	2	3	4	5	6	7
2. Are there evidences of joy and happiness?	1	2	3	4	5	6	7
3. Is there peace, oneness, and unity?	1	2	3	4	5	6	7
4. Are believers showing patience with each other?	1	2	3	4	5	6	7
5. Are they kind in their actions and attitudes?	1	2	3	4	5	6	7
6. Are they demonstrating goodness? (This is done through concrete acts rather than only words.)	1	2	3	4	5	6	7
7. Are they faithful to each	1	2	3	4	5	6	7

other? (This is the opposite
of being fickle and untrust-
worthy.)

8. Are they demonstrating   1   2   3   4   5   6   7
gentleness and sensitivity
in their relationships with
each other?

9. Is there self-control in   1   2   3   4   5   6   7
their conversations with
each other and in their
general lifestyle?

Some Christians do not believe the "acts of the old nature" are
visible in their church because there is no flagrant sexual immorality, impurity, debauchery, idolatry, witchcraft, drunkenness, and
orgies. But they conveniently overlook the fact that the "acts of the
old nature" also include hatred, discord, jealousy, fits of rage, selfish ambition, dissension, factions, and envy.

If you have difficulty recognizing these positive reflections of
Jesus Christ among church members, there can be but one conclu-
sion: more "acts of the sinful nature" are being reflected than the
"fruit of the Spirit." When this is true, Christians are not actively
"serving one another in love." Rather, they are "serving one another" in sinful, unselfish ways.

Step 2

*In order to check your own objectivity and the accuracy of your observa-
tions, ask several Christians in your church to take Step 1.* Then prayerfully compare notes.

Step 3

*If your group feels others in your church are not actively "serving one
another in love," if the "acts of the sinful nature" are more obvious than
"the fruit of the Spirit,"* think about taking the following approaches:

First, make sure you are not guilty of allowing your old nature
to dominate your own relationships with others.

Second, as a small group, commit to modeling among yourselves the fruit of the Spirit to others in the church.

Third, begin to pray for others in the church—but only after you've made sure your own lives are in order.

Fourth, carefully guard against "spiritual pride" and "pseudo-spirituality." Attitudes of superiority and spiritual pride create more problems than solutions.

DISCUSSION GUIDE FOR SMALL GROUPS

OPENING

Welcome one another with the group greeting you developed last time. Then have each person share a response to this question: If you could have a servant devoted to only one task, what task would you assign that person?

FOR DISCUSSION

1. Read Galatians 5:13. What is the relationship between freedom and serving others? What parallels do you see between being a servant of Jesus and a servant to others?

2. What are Christians free from? How do you experience this in your own life?

3. What are some specific ways that Christians can "serve one another"? How does the fruit of the Spirit (Gal. 5:22-23) relate to serving one another?

4. Together, compare your evaluations of the evidence of the fruit of the Spirit in your church, using step 1 of the "Practical Steps." In what areas do you see cause for concern? In what specific ways can your small group consciously attempt to demonstrate the fruit of the Spirit?

CLOSING

In pairs, share your personal needs for growth in demonstrating the fruit of the Spirit, and then pray for each other. Then pray for your church as a whole.

For Next Time

1. Read chapter 9.
2. Continue to pray for your church.
3. Consciously look for ways to demonstrate the fruit of the Spirit in your relationships this week—particularly in your family setting.

 *Chapter Nine*

Carrying One Another's Burdens

Carry each other's burdens, and in this way you will
fulfill the law of Christ.

Galatians 6:2

One Sunday morning I was handed the shock of my life. I was in the middle of one of our services at church and someone reported to me that a good friend of mine had left his wife and six children and had moved into an apartment with his neighbor's wife. I couldn't believe my ears! How could this be? This man was well known as a stalwart believer—a former missionary and now a successful Christian businessman! His name appeared as a board member with several well-known Christian organizations. It had to be some mistake!

Unfortunately, it was not a mistake. Since I had finished teaching, I actually turned the service over to one of my fellow pastors, contacted one of our elders who knew this man well—and together we made our way to his home. When we arrived, I found this man's wife in tears and his six children sitting on the floor—ranging in ages from very young to teenagers. The neighbor woman's husband was also there. He had obviously drunk too much—his way of dealing with the grief. I tried to minister to this family—

then decided with my fellow elder that we would do our best to confront this man the next day at his place of business.

When we arrived, my friend was anything but in a receptive mood. He asked us to leave his office, stating that he had made up his mind—something that he had been thinking about for a long time. I responded by telling him as lovingly as possible that we weren't leaving because we loved him too much to allow him to proceed on this disastrous course!

Finally, he consented to talk to us outside the building. Since his office was glassed in on all sides, our visit wasn't unnoticed by the other employees. They knew something was terribly wrong. Sensing we were serious about not leaving, he consented to talk in a more private place.

That day I told my friend something I have never told anyone since. As he continued to put pressure on us to leave, in my intensity I told him he would have to deck me on the concrete pavement since we were not leaving. Again, in a rather elevated voice, I reassured him that we were there because we loved him and wanted to help set him free from this horrible sin trap that he had fallen into. Later, my fellow elder told me that he was standing behind me literally shaking—especially since the gentleman we were confronting was much more robust and physical than we were. He could have easily followed through on my suggestion.

Once again—seeing how determined we were—he finally consented to go to a quiet place to talk. Sitting in the back of a restaurant in a very private booth, we once again pleaded for him to go for counseling. I will never forget my fellow elder reaching out and putting his hand on my friend's arm and with tears in his eyes, pleading with him to go for help. We told him we would go with him.

Again, seeing we were not about to leave—and after about two hours of intense communication—he finally agreed to see a Christian counselor. We went with him and his wife. In that meeting, he decided to go for six weeks of counseling. Later, he told me that he had agreed to our suggestions only to "get us off his back."

Approximately six weeks went by and I hadn't seen or talked with this man. However, I knew he was in counseling. He kept his word. And then one day, while I was leading the Sunday service, I looked up—and to my pleasant surprise—he walked in with his wife and sat down. After the service he made his way to the front, put his big arms around me and with tears streaming down his cheeks he said, "Gene, thank God you didn't let me go!"

Obviously, the Lord worked a miracle in this man's life. He had another eight wonderful years of marriage before his wife died of cancer. Since then, he has been remarried to a wonderful Christian woman and is still walking in the Lord's will. He has heard me tell this story several times—and each time has responded with tears and a deep sense of appreciation. On one occasion, he said, "I'll be indebted to you the rest of my life."

A TRUE TEST OF LOVE

Dealing with sin in the lives of fellow believers is one of the most difficult tasks God has given Christians. It's much easier to carry out the other "one another" injunctions. However, tough love is much more difficult. I dread it every time, primarily because of the double emotional whammy. First, I don't relish intruding into another person's private life. It always makes me uncomfortable. Second, I always fear rejection—which is painful. However, I've discovered the true test of love for another Christian is whether I am willing to take this kind of risk. Furthermore, it's the true test of my love for God—whether or not I am willing to obey His will in spite of my uncomfortable emotional reactions.

Many churches ignore this responsibility entirely. Others treat it lightly. Still others deal with the issue of sin only after it has created a scandal that can't be ignored. Unfortunately by then, it's usually too late to help the person who has been trapped in sin. There is too much pain, hurt, misunderstanding, embarrassment and resentment.

When Paul wrote to the Galatian Christians, he was concerned that this not happen. He exhorted these believers to "carry each other's burdens" (Gal. 6:2). The "burden" Paul was addressing was the heavy load that weighs us down when we are in bondage to sin. This should not surprise us, since he had just discussed in detail what it means to keep in step with the Spirit and "serve one another in love" rather than to become slaves to "the acts of the sinful nature."

Paul came right to the point—

Brothers, *if someone is caught in a sin*, you who are spiritual should restore him gently. But watch yourself, or you also may be tempted (Gal. 6:1).

Paul left no questions about this issue. Christians *do* have a responsibility when others sin. We have no choice if we want to be in God's will. We are to attempt to restore that person—to help him acknowledge his sin and overcome it.

To accomplish this goal, Paul gave some specific guidelines for carrying out this process—guidelines that are absolutely essential if there are to be positive results.

RESTORATION IS A TASK FOR SPIRITUAL CHRISTIANS

Generally speaking, there are two classes of people described in the New Testament: Christians and non-Christians. But there are also two classes of Christians: "spiritual" and "worldly"—or "unspiritual." Spiritual Christians are those who "live by the Spirit" and who "keep in step with the Spirit" (Gal. 5:25). We can recognize these believers because they manifest the fruit of the Spirit in their relationships with one another: love, joy, peace, patience, kindness, goodness, faithfulness, gentleness, and self-control (Gal. 5:22-23).

What areis a "worldly" Christians? They are definitely believers, but sometimes it's difficult to tell. They often live like non-Christians—indulging in "the acts of the sinful nature." The Corinthians definitely fit this category. Paul knew they were true believers because he had seen evidences of God's grace in their lives (1 Cor. 1:4-7). He even identified them as "those sanctified in Christ Jesus" (1:2a), and as believers who had also been "called to be holy" (1:2b). Unfortunately, they had made very little progress in this area of their lives. In Christ, God saw them as "holy" the moment they were born again—something that is true for every Christian and the only reason we can be saved. But in terms of daily Christian living, they were not reflecting who God is—a holy, righteous, and eternal being.

Paul went on to say that after he had led them to Christ and lived among them, he could not talk to them as *spiritual*, but as *worldly* believers. Listen to Paul as he described their lifestyle:

> Brothers, I could not address you as spiritual but as world-ly—mere infants in Christ. I gave you milk, not solid food, for you were not yet ready for it. Indeed, you are still not ready. You are still worldly. For since there is jealousy and quarrel-ing among you, are you not worldly? Are you not acting like mere men? [*that is, as non-Christians*] (1 Cor. 3:1-3).

Paul's description of the Corinthians' behavior here and in the rest of this letter correlates with what he described in his Galatian letter as the "acts of the sinful nature." They were still "walking in the flesh" rather than "in the Spirit." Their relationships with each other were anything but reflections of the Holy Spirit's guidance and fruit.

Paul exhorted the Galatian Christians to help people like this. But he made it clear that dealing with sin in the life of a worldly Christian is not a task for Christians who are also living out of the will of God. Rather, he wrote, "You who are *spiritual* should restore him" (Gal. 6:1).

All of the "one another" exhortations we have looked at thus far indicate that all Christians are responsible to minister to each other. However, only those in the body of Christ who are relatively mature are to deal with serious sin in the lives of other believers. This is why Jesus spoke so pointedly about this matter:

> Can a blind man lead a blind man? Will they not both fall into a pit? . . . Why do you look at the speck of sawdust in your brother's eye and pay no attention to the plank in your own eye? How can you say to your brother, "Brother, let me take the speck out of your eye," when you yourself fail to see

the plank in your own eye? You hypocrite, first take the plank out of your eye, and then you will see clearly to remove the speck from your brother's eye (Luke 6:39, 41-42).

Spiritual Christians, then, have a definite responsibility to help worldly Christians—especially those who are "caught in a sin." But even further, we have a responsibility to avoid causing them to sin. Paul wrote to the Romans:

> We who are strong ought to bear with the failings of the weak and not to please ourselves. Each of us should please his neighbor for his good, to build him up (Rom. 15:1-2; see also 1 Cor. 8:9).

RESTORATION IS A TASK FOR MORE THAN ONE PERSON

There are two types of sinful behavior outlined in Scripture calling for two different approaches for dealing with that sin. First, there is the person who sins against another brother or sister in Christ. Second, there is the person who sins against himself and the larger body of Christ.

Sin Against Another Christian

Jesus Christ outlined a very specific approach for dealing with this kind of sin:

> If your brother sins against you, go and show him his fault, just between the two of you. If he listens to you, you have won your brother over. But if he will not listen, take one or two others along, so that "every matter may be established by the testimony of two or three witnesses." If he refuses to listen to them, tell it to the church; and if he refuses to listen even to the church, treat him as you would a pagan or a tax collector (Matt. 18:15-17).

Here Jesus specifically outlined the procedure for handling sin in the lives of someone who has sinned against another Christian on a personal basis. In such cases, confrontation should also be one-on-one. With the exception of seeking wisdom from another mature Christian regarding how to proceed, we are not to talk to others but to go directly to the person who has sinned against us. However, if this person will not listen, then we are to take several others with us to once again confront the problem. Again, if there is no response, we're to take the matter to "the church"—which in most instances, involves the spiritual leaders. If there is still no response, we have no recourse but to relate to this person as if he were a non-Christian—even though he may be a believer.

A Christian Who Is Trapped in Sin

Paul was dealing with this kind of sin in Galatians. In this case, a Christian is in bondage to sin and needs help. His sin is against himself and the larger family of God. In these instances, Paul indicates that this person should be approached by several spiritual Christians immediately. Thus, he wrote: "You [plural] who are spiritual should restore him."

In some respects, Paul actually picked up with the third step outlined by Jesus. This approach would include the individual who refuses to listen to his offended brother or sister, and also refuses to listen to two or three witnesses. At this point, several "spiritual" Christians are to attempt to rescue this person and to set him free from this trap. That's what another elder and I attempted to do for my friend who was trapped in adultery. In this case, he had refused to listen to his wife and his children.

Restoration Is to Be Done with Genuine Humility

"Restore him gently!" wrote Paul. In essence, he was referring to meekness and humility. Thus, he wrote later: "If anyone thinks he is something when he is nothing, he deceives himself" (Gal. 6:1, 3). Thank God, he responded.

WE ARE ALL OBJECTS OF GOD'S GRACE

Christians who approach another Christian about sin must do so with a great sense of their own unworthiness to be called children of

God. In fact, Paul made it clear to Titus that we are also to approach non-Christians in this way—"To show true humility toward all men." Then he explained why:

> At one time we too were foolish, disobedient, deceived and enslaved [*trapped*] by all kinds of passions and pleasures We lived in malice and envy, being hated and hating one another. But when the kindness and love of God our Savior appeared, he saved, us, not because of righteous things we had done, but because of his mercy (Titus 3:2-5).

Paul was exhorting Titus to remind the Christians at Crete to approach everyone with a true sense of understanding, meekness, and humility. We must always remember that it is only God's grace that has saved us when we were yet in our sins. No saved person who truly understands the grace of God in his own life can approach any person (saved or unsaved) with arrogance, pride, or a sense of superiority.

This was Paul's concern when writing to the Galatians regarding how to help Christians who were "caught in a sin." He admonished spiritual believers to approach those people with an attitude of true gentleness and humility. With this approach, they would help carry that person's burden with the same attitude Christ had toward us while we were yet in our sins. This is why Paul himself appealed to the Corinthians—Christians who were trapped in many sins—"By the meekness and gentleness of Christ" (2 Cor. 10:1).

This is also why Paul warned Timothy to avoid getting into quarrels with people who were opposing the truth of God. Rather, anyone who wants to serve God, Paul wrote:

> Must be kind to everyone, able to teach, not resentful. Those who oppose him he must gently instruct [*with patience and humility*], in the hope that God will grant them repentance leading them to a knowledge of the truth, and that they will come to their senses and escape from the trap of the devil, who has taken them captive to do his will (2 Tim. 2:24-26).

We've all made mistakes in dealing with sin in the lives of other Christians—as a parent with our children, as a pastor with our people, or as one Christian with another. Personally, I've had the best response confronting those who are out of fellowship with God when I've acted in harmony with Paul's injunctions to treat others with gentleness, humility, and meekness. I've had my most negative responses when I have been insensitive, too quick to judge, and too harsh with my words. I may have been *right* in my observations regarding sin, but *wrong* in the way I went about seeking to correct the person.

WHEN WORLDLY CHRISTIANS WILL NOT RESPOND POSITIVELY

No matter how gentle, kind, sensitive, and humble we are, there are some worldly Christians who will not respond to this approach. Paul saw this possibility when he wrote to the Corinthians. Consequently, he gave them a choice. "What do you prefer?" he asked. "Shall I come to you with a whip, or in love and with a gentle spirit?" (1 Cor. 4:21).

Some Christians are so caught up in their sins, so self-deceived, and so arrogant that they will not respond to a gentle, humble approach. If they do not, we must then take a second step in church discipline—to break fellowship with that kind of believer.

Because of the immature way the Corinthians had responded to sinfulness in the church, Paul pulled no punches:

> But now I am writing you that you must not associate with anyone who calls himself a brother but is sexually immoral or greedy, an idolater or a slanderer, a drunkard or a swindler. With such a man do not even eat (1 Cor. 5:11).

This was the final step for Paul. However, his tough love brought unusual results. The Corinthians dealt with the man in their midst who was living in flagrant immorality. They also came to grips with their own sins. As Paul wrote in his second letter: "Godly sorrow brings repentance . . . See what this godly sorrow has produced in you" (2 Cor. 7:10-11). Furthermore, the immoral man who had been expelled from their midst also became repentant. In Christlike fashion, Paul exhorted them to forgive the man, to receive him back, to love him, and to encourage him in the Christian faith (2 Cor. 2:5-8). As always, restoration is the true purpose for discipline—not ultimate alienation.

On one occasion, a Christian man swindled several fellow believers in a business deal. He actually violated federal laws—and then denied his wrongdoing. Several men met to lovingly but directly confront him with his sins.

Initially, he seemed repentant. However, his subsequent behavior indicated he had not responded with a spirit of true brokenness and sorrow. He continued to manipulate and lie. Those who were victims of his deceptive practices continued to report this behavior to the leaders in the church. As the net continued to close in on him, this man wrote a letter to the elders attacking the people who were trying to bring this problem to the surface. Incidentally, this is a common tactic on the part of guilty people who will not admit sin. They often attempt to draw attention away from themselves by putting the blame on others.

At this point, the problem went beyond Paul's guidelines for restoration in Galatians 6:1-2. This man rejected help. Consequently, the leaders in the church had to move to the final step in Jesus' plan—to take the matter "to the church." In this case, the "church" was represented by the elders and all the offended parties. There was no need—there never is—to involve the "whole church" unless *everyone* is affected.

Unfortunately, when this man was confronted by the elders and all the offended parties, he still did not respond with total honesty and repentance. Though he admitted to some lying and criminal activity, he would not follow through with the elders' suggestion to turn himself in to the proper authorities. Rather, he chose to leave the church.

At this point, the spiritual leaders and the offended parties could do nothing but treat this man as an unbeliever—not that he was actually a non-Christian. Rather, with the authority of Jesus Christ, they had to treat him as they would treat a non-Christian who had engaged in the same kind of deceptive and illegal activities. Consequently, the only recourse for the people who had been swindled was to take the matter to legal authorities who are set up to deal with such cases. It's unfortunate when we have to go before pagan courts but when a Christian will not respond to loving confrontation as it's outlined in Scripture, we have no alternative plan. The Christian who violates the laws of the state must suffer the consequences.

RESTORATION MUST BE DONE CAUTIOUSLY

When several Christians, even spiritual Christians, approach someone to help him escape from the trap of sin, it must be done carefully. "Watch yourself," warned Paul. "You also may be tempted" (Gal. 6:1).

This is another reason why it's important to have more than one person involved in this kind of confrontation and intervention. The lusts of the flesh are very deceptive—and very attractive. Some Christians, when attempting to help another believer who is trapped in some sin, may fall into the same sin.

I have a pastor friend who fell into this trap. He was trying to help a woman who had a bad relationship with her husband. You can guess what happened. He ended up in a sexual relationship with this person. Though he confessed his sin, it had a devastating impact on his wife and family. Though there has been restoration and forgiveness, the scars are still evident—and probably will be for the rest of their lives.

RESTORATION MUST BE DONE PRAYERFULLY

James adds an important dimension to the process involved in bearing the sin burdens of other Christians. "Confess your sins to each other," he wrote in his epistle. Then he spelled out why: "And pray for each other so that you may be healed" (James 5:16).

When a Christian indulges in sin, when he "sows to please his sinful nature," he will from that nature "reap destruction" (Gal. 6:7-8). Obviously, a non-Christian who does not turn to Christ but continues in his sin will end up spending eternity without Christ. But "destruction" also involves Christians who do not "keep in step with the Spirit," but rather "indulge in the acts of the sinful nature."

There is inevitable deterioration in their lives—spiritually, psychologically, and physically.

James indicates that some Christians—not all—are physically ill because of sin.

> Is any one of you sick? He should call the elders of the church to pray over him and anoint him with oil in the name of the Lord. And the prayer offered in faith will make the sick person well; the Lord will raise him up. If he has sinned, he will be forgiven. Therefore confess your sins to each other and pray for each other so that you may be healed (James 5:14-16).

Note again that James does not say that all illness is caused by specific sin. Rather, he wrote, "If he *has sinned,* he will be forgiven" (5:15).

God, of course, does not promise to heal all believers when we have physical and psychological illnesses. However, He does honor obedience and faith. And in many instances, when we pray according to His will, He will in fact heal. Sometimes this happens in very dramatic ways!

One thing is certain. If we confess our sins, the blood of Jesus Christ continues to cleanse us from all sin (1 John 1:9). No matter what we have done that violates the will of God, there is always forgiveness. We may suffer the consequences of those sins in our physical and emotional lives—but this is not because we have not received forgiveness.

PRACTICAL STEPS FOR APPLYING THIS PRINCIPLE TODAY

Step 1

Always evaluate your own life before trying to help another Christian who is trapped in sin.

Are you among those who are spiritual? That is, are you ordering your life by the Spirit, keeping in step with the Spirit? Are you living in such a way, and in relationship to other Christians, that the fruit of the Spirit is obvious in your life?

Check yourself! If you classify yourself among those who are

spiritual, you will reflect love and joy; you will be at peace with
other Christians; you will demonstrate patience, kindness, goodness, faithfulness, gentleness, and self-control (Gal. 5:22-23).

And whatever you do, remember Jesus' words. In essence, He
said, "Don't try to take the speck of sawdust out of your brother's
eye when you have a two-by-four in your own" (see Matt. 7:4).

Step 2

*Always evaluate another Christian's lifestyle from a truly biblical per-
spective.*

Unfortunately, some Christians go around looking for sin in
other Christians' lives. Some are expert at making up "extrabiblical" lists to help them evaluate sins. This, of course, can quickly lead to judging others (see Rom. 14:13), which is sin in itself. It
reflects a pharisaical attitude.

On the other hand, Christians are to be concerned for those
Christians who become trapped in some sin. Not surprisingly, just
before Paul admonished Christians to "carry each other's burdens," he
cataloged the "acts of the sinful nature" (Gal. 5:19-21). This list in turn
becomes a biblical criterion for determining what is indeed sin in a
believer's life. This is a supracultural list, a guideline for all time.

Following are four lists, representing four translations. All these
are included to enable you to discover more specific definitions of
what Paul listed. Some of the Greek words he used tend to be general and interrelated. The four viewpoints will help you determine
more accurately what Paul was saying.

KJV	NIV	NASB	BECK
adultery and fornication	sexual immorality	immorality	sexual sin
uncleanness	impurity	impurity	uncleanness
lasciviousness	debauchery	sensuality	wild living
idolatry	idolatry	idolatry	worshiping of idols
witchcraft	witchcraft	sorcery	witchcraft
hatred	hatred	enmities	hate
variance	discord	strife	wrangling

emulations	jealousy	jealousy	jealousy
wrath	fits of rage	outbursts of anger	anger
strife	selfish ambition	disputes	selfishness
seditions	dissensions	dissensions	quarreling
heresies	factions	factions	divisions
envyings, murders	envy	envying	envy
drunkenness	drunkenness	drunkenness	drunkenness
revellings	orgies	carousing	carousing

Step 3

Always follow biblical procedures when confronting Christians trapped in sin.

The New Testament outlines three levels of disciplinary action.

First, we are to warn a Christian about his sin, attempting to restore him and release him from Satan's trap (1 Thes. 5:14; Gal. 6:1-2).

Second, if a person does not respond and turn from his sin, then we are not to fellowship with that Christian (2 Thes. 3:6, 14).

The final step is excommunication—to actually consider this person as if he were an unbeliever (Matt. 18:17).

It has been my experience that when we follow proper procedure in dealing with sin in the lives of other Christians, it is seldom necessary to go beyond the first level. Either the person responds and repents, or chooses to separate from fellow Christians without being asked. This is particularly true when we speak the truth in love. Even though people don't respond positively, they appreciate the concern and choose to leave the church rather than creating more problems.

Unfortunately, it is at the initial level that we frequently fail to act. Furthermore, it is this first level that Paul had in mind when he said we are to "carry each other's burdens" in order to set them free from sin. Restoration should be the true purpose of all discipline, no matter on what level we're operating. Discipline must always be done in love and with the purpose of helping the person turn from his sin and to once again "keep in step with the Spirit" rather than engaging in "the acts of the sinful nature."

DISCUSSION GUIDE FOR SMALL GROUPS

OPENING

Read aloud the opening illustration in this chapter. Then, discuss the following questions:

If you were confronted with this problem, how would you respond?

How can we know how much pressure to put on a person who doesn't respond initially?

Why will this approach not always work?

What biblical guidelines are reflected in this illustration?

FOR DISCUSSION

1. What kind of "burdens" first come to mind when you think of "carrying each other's burdens"? Read Galatians 6:1-2. What indications do you see that "carrying each other's burdens" refers to restoring someone who is caught in a sin?

2. What's the difference between being "caught in a sin" (Gal. 6:1) and simply living a worldly life? Look at the list of sins on the previous two pages. Which of these sins would you immediately consider cause for confrontation? How would you determine when some of the other sins (for example, jealousy) were serious enough to call for confrontation? How do you make this decision without being judgmental?

3. Read Galatians 6:5. How does this statement relate to the instruction to "carry each other's burdens"? How does it relate to the qualifications for being a burden-bearer?

4. What needs to happen to make "carrying each other's burdens" a reality in your church?

CLOSING

While studying this chapter, some group members may have recognized a responsibility to approach someone about a sin. To provide a safe, confidential environment for those group members to find support, form pairs. Let individuals share the situation in confidence, without naming names, with their partners. Have partners pray for each other and the person caught in sin, and identify ways to support each other in this responsibility. If people do not have specific situations in which they feel they need to confront others, encourage them to pray for each other's continued growth as spiritual, humble Christians.

For Next Time

1. Read chapter 10.
2. Continue to pray for your partner and anyone you know who is caught in a sin. *1-6-13*

1. *Neil - Bach*
2. *Marye*
3. *Archie*
4. *Terry*
5. *Pam - Tue - Chemo* *1-29-13* *4 more treatments left*
6. *Doug H. New - Family*
7. *Annette Chin*
8. *Katy* *1-13-13*
9.

1. *Marye.*
2. *Frances*
3. *Chris Smith*
4. *Bennett Burke*
5. *w/ ayps thoughts*

Chapter Ten

Bear with One Another

Be completely humble and gentle; be patient, bearing
with one another in love.

Ephesians 4:2

I really enjoy people. Since I have a pretty good picture of my own
weaknesses, I find it rather easy to tolerate those weaknesses in others. In that sense, I am fortunate. Some people have the most difficulty accepting the weaknesses in others that remind them of the
same weaknesses in themselves.

Yet, as I reflect on my past and present relationships, a few
faces come to mind—people who have been very difficult to
accept and love.

One such face comes to mind. This man was his own worst
enemy—and still is. He has always been at odds with someone.
Ironically, he knows—and has admitted—that he has a way of rub-
bing people the wrong way. But sadly, he just doesn't change.

I remember one time he came into my office and unloaded
on me personally—and several other people. I listened to his
tirade without comment for about forty-five minutes. He then
got up to leave. At that point, I informed him that I had lis-

tened patiently to his accusations and asked him for the cour-
tesy to respond.

To his credit, he obliged as I took the next thirty minutes to
answer his charges one by one. Fortunately, I had a fellow pastor
with me, who also knew him well. When I finished, he picked up
where I left off, confirmed what I had said, and then shared some
additional things this man needed to hear.

At this point, he became humble and submissive. Frankly, I really believe he was sincere. He tore up his notes—and told me he
would never bring up those issues again.

But, unfortunately, the change was temporary. He soon reverted
to his old habits of being critical and judgmental. Recently, I have
seen him unmercifully attack another spiritual leader and without
cause. Of all the men I know, this pastor does not deserve this kind
of diatribe.

I still love this cantankerous man—and periodically pray for
him—but frankly, I don't miss being around him. I know I have forgiven him for his rudeness, his insensitive spirit, and his judgmental attitudes. In a sense, I believe I am "bearing with him in love."
And I truly hope he changes. I know for sure it will be a great blessing to his wife and his children. In the meantime, I readily admit
I'm not unhappy to share the responsibility with someone else to
be used of the Lord to bring him to repentance and to help him
reflect the fruit of the Spirit in his life.

I share this story—not to dump on this man—but to simply
share that there are Christians who are difficult to love. In reality, they are having difficulty "loving themselves." Fortunately,
few are as difficult to be around as this man. Most people
respond to loving confrontation. They change. But when they
don't, we are still to "bear with them in love"—which may mean
additional confrontations.

PATIENCE

When it comes to dealing with each other's weaknesses, Paul made
our responsibility to one another even clearer in his Letter to the
Colossians:

Therefore, as God's chosen people, holy and dearly loved, clothe yourselves with compassion, kindness, humility, gentleness and patience. Bear with each other and forgive whatever grievances you may have against one another. Forgive as the Lord forgave you (Col. 3:12-13).

Several key words precede Paul's injunction to "bear with one another"—"compassion, kindness, gentleness and patience." However, the key word is "patience."

The *King James Version* uses the word "longsuffering," one aspect of "walking in the Spirit" (Gal. 5:25). Patience is also the focus of Paul's prayer for these New Testament Christians:

And we pray this . . . so that you may have great endurance and patience, and joyfully giving thanks to the Father, who has qualified you to share in the inheritance of the saints in the kingdom of light (Col. 1:10-12).

To "bear with one another," then means being patient with each other's weaknesses. Not one of us is perfect. All of us fail, particularly in human relationships. How easy it is to expect more from other Christians than we expect from ourselves!

This is particularly true in our families. In this setting, we get to know one another as in no other social unit. We live together day after day, week after week, year after year. It's a "wall-to-wall" experience. In this setting, we are seen at our best and at our worst— both as parents and as children. Parents often expect more from their children than they do from themselves. Children often expect more from their parents than from other adults in their lives. Together, this dynamic often erupts in anything but patience and forbearance with one another.

The same is true of our extended family. As we "live together" as brothers and sisters in Christ, we get to know each other's idiosyncrasies. We are then faced with the challenge to "bear with one another in love." When we are tempted to be impatient with one another, we need to think about Jesus Christ and His attitude toward us. This was Paul's motivation. The Lord's long-suffering and patience toward this man marked his life and gave him unusual tolerance toward others (1 Tim. 1:15-17). Seeing himself as the worst of sinners and experiencing God's love and patience in saving him caused Paul to respond to others with the love and patience of Jesus Christ.

A FORGIVING SPIRIT

"Bearing with one another" and having a "forgiving spirit" are synonymous in God's sight. Note again how Paul made this clear in his Letter to the Colossians. "Bear with each other," he said, "and *forgive* whatever grievances you may have against one another. *Forgive* as the Lord forgave you" (Col. 3:13).

Some Christians carry grudges for years. How miserable! How tragic! And how out of character for a follower of Jesus Christ. How ungrateful for a Christian to hold a grudge against a fellow believer when Christ has canceled our own debt of sin.

Recently I received a letter from a fellow pastor who admitted that he had been carrying feelings of bitterness toward me. He asked forgiveness—which I was quick to give. In actuality, I had forgiven him long before but it was a great blessing to see that God had convicted him for his attitude. To his credit, he was preparing a message from Scripture on the subject of forgiveness and responded to conviction from the Holy Spirit. What a relief to let him know I had already forgiven him and would continue to pray for his ministry.

A POWERFUL STORY

One day Peter came to Jesus and asked, "Lord, how many times shall I forgive my brother when he sins against me? Up to seven times?"

"Jesus answered, 'I tell you, not seven times, but seventy-seven times'" (Matt. 18:21-22).

Jesus then told a story to get his point across:

Therefore, the kingdom of heaven is like a king who wanted to settle accounts with his servants. As he began the settlement, a man who owed him ten thousand talents was brought to him. Since he was not able to pay, the master ordered that he and his wife and his children and all that he had be sold to repay the debt.

The servant fell on his knees before him. "Be patient with me," he begged, "and I will pay back everything." The servant's master took pity on him, canceled the debt and let him go.

But when that servant went out, he found one of his fellow servants who owed him a hundred denarii. He grabbed him and began to choke him. "Pay back what you owe me!" he demanded.

His fellow servant fell to his knees and begged him, "Be patient with me, and I will pay you back."

But he refused. Instead, he went off and had the man thrown into prison until he could pay the debt. When the other servants saw what had happened, they were greatly distressed and went and told their master all that had happened.

Then the master called the servant in. "You wicked servant," he said, "I canceled all that debt of yours because you begged me to. Shouldn't you have had mercy on your fellow servant just as I had on you?" In anger his master turned him over to the jailers to be tortured, until he should pay back all he owed.

This is how My heavenly Father will treat each of you unless you forgive your brother from your heart (Matt. 18:23-35).

"MAKE EVERY EFFORT!"

Immediately following Paul's exhortation to "be patient, bearing with one another in love," he said, "*Make every effort* to keep the unity of the Spirit through the bond of peace" (Eph. 4:2-3).

Patience, forbearance, and forgiveness are not automatic actions that follow conversion to Christ. They are deliberate acts of the will. Every person I know who has an unforgiving spirit chooses to do so. I know this is true in my own life. We often choose to let the other person know how we feel—by avoiding that person, by using cutting and sharp words, by talking behind a person's back.

On the other hand, Christians who really care about each other, who are really concerned about doing the will of God at all times, will "make every effort to keep the unity of the Spirit through the bond of peace." This is Christianity in action.

On one occasion, someone told me I deeply offended another brother in Christ. He believed I had purposely passed by him without "saying hello." Frankly, I was shocked. I know myself well enough to know that I didn't do this on purpose. In fact, I have difficulty even avoiding people I know don't like me, let alone someone I love and respect—which is how I felt about this brother.

However, even though this person had moved to another part of the country, I picked up the telephone, called him, and apologized. I told him I had heard via the grapevine that he felt that I had snubbed him. I apologized, stating that sometimes I get preoccupied—which is not an excuse—and inadvertently pass by people without speaking. I'm confident that's what must have happened. He quickly forgave me and admitted his own supersensitivity. Thank God I was able to restore this relationship—even though I didn't know it was broken. I'm thankful that someone cared enough to alert me to this problem.

HUSBANDS AND WIVES

Probably the greatest challenge we face as married people is to bear with one another's weaknesses. It's at this level that we get to know each other in ways that other people don't.

Unfortunately, some couples don't learn to communicate with each other regarding the things that irritate them. Sometimes these begin as little things that mushroom into gigantic irritants. Then comes the explosion—and it often comes as a surprise to the mate who has created the problem.

At times, these things happen simply because we bottle up our feelings and don't share what's bothering us. At other times, our communication is so minimal that the other person doesn't hear us. For example, in my own marriage, I remember situations where my wife was trying to tell me something. However, by her own admission, her "transmission" was so weak that I missed the message completely. On my side, my "receiver" was turned down so low that I couldn't have heard the "signal" even if it had been coming through. When we have this kind of problem—particularly on both sides of the relationship—it should not surprise us that there is going to be a breakdown in communication.

Open and clear communication is absolutely essential to enable us to "bear with one another in love." Furthermore, once we understand what irritates our mate, we need to set definite goals to change those things. For example, I discovered that it irritated my wife for me to leave the shower door covered with water. She finally told me she was tired of mopping down the door after it dried and left spots that took a lot of work to remove. Once I understood the problem, I solved it. True, it took me awhile to establish the habit—but now it's automatic. In a matter of seconds, I can use the towel to do something that pleases my wife.

I also have a friend that admitted he had a very bad habit of leaving the dresser drawers half open. It irritated his wife that she had to come after him and close the drawers. Finally, after a period of time, he got the message—and realized how important it was to learn to be thoughtful in this area. Furthermore, it only took a second to close those drawers. Think of what this little act of kindness did to eliminate tension.

It's true that some people are overly demanding. It seems we can never please them. When this happens in marriage, a couple is headed for serious trouble. However, it should not continue to happen among Christians. We of all people ought to be able to "carry our own load" in a relationship (Gal. 6:5). When each of us loves the other as Christ loved us, the problem will inevitably be resolved.

PARENTS AND CHILDREN

Parents face this same problem with children—only to a greater degree. Unfortunately, small children don't understand reciprocal relationships. They're naturally self-centered until they reach certain levels of maturation.

As parents, then, we must be very careful not to expect too much from small children. If we do, we'll only frustrate them and create anger and resentment and greater problems. This is why Paul wrote, "Fathers, do not embitter your children, or they will become discouraged" (Col. 3:21).

I'm often amazed at the way some parents expect their children to measure up to standards they do not practice themselves. Obviously, this will indeed lead to anger, bitterness, and discouragement. Children read hypocrisy very clearly.

Children, of course, must learn to practice this principle. However, they learn best by seeing it practiced by their parents—in a relationship with one another—and with them. They then have a basis for understanding what it really means when we tell them to be patient and forgiving—in short, "to bear with one another in love."

PASTOR AND PEOPLE

As I stated earlier, I love people and have little difficulty relating to them. But there is one area I become impatient and have to watch my attitude. For example, I try to model generosity. My wife and I tithe regularly to our church (give 10 percent of our gross income) and we always try to be first to support special projects and to give beyond our tithe. We've built this into our lifestyle over the years and don't spend money on our "wants" unless we first set aside money for the Lord's work.

However, it's no secret we live in a materialistic culture—and it has infected Christians. Frankly, it bothers me when I see Christians being selfish with their money—and letting other Christians carry the financial burden for the church. Yet, these same people "selfishly" enjoy all the benefits of the church—the benefits that other people have provided.

Please don't misunderstand. I'm not talking about people who can't give because of financial difficulties. I'm talking about Christians who pay their television cable bills regularly, sport their mobile phones, go out to eat regularly, and take in movies once or twice a week—and yet don't support the Lord's work. I'm speaking of Christians who put away savings every month, drive two or three expensive cars, take expensive vacation trips and yet don't share their excess with the Lord.

Yes, these people bother me—especially when they know what the Bible teaches about being generous. However, my Bible teaches me that I must "bear with these people in love." I must continue to model and teach them, realizing that only the Holy Spirit can ultimately change their lives. It's at this point I must learn to be patient and forgiving—not allowing their weaknesses to keep me from being a loving Christian.

PRACTICAL STEPS FOR
BEARING WITH ONE ANOTHER IN LOVE
Step 1

Take a good look at yourself.

In all honesty, make a list of your weaknesses and idiosyncrasies. These questions will help you.

1. What do I do (or not do) at home that irritates my wife and children (or my parents, my brothers, and my sisters, or apartment-mate)?

2. What do I do (or not do) at church that irritates my fellow brothers and sisters in Christ?

3. What do I do (or not do) at work and/or school that irritates fellow employees and/or teachers and fellow students?

4. What do I do (or not do) that irritates my friends?

Step 2

Evaluate your weaknesses in the light of your attitudes and actions toward other Christians.

The following questions will help you:

Do you expect more from others than you do from yourself?

Do you criticize others in the area of your own weaknesses?

Step 3

Make a list of all Christians you have difficulty relating to.

If you can't think of anyone, praise the Lord! Don't drudge up names just to have something to write about. But make sure you're being honest.

Once you have made a list, ask yourself *why* you can't relate to these Christians. Why are you angry at them? Is it because of something they have done to hurt you? Are they aware of how you feel? Are your feelings justified? Or, are you feeling the way you do simply because of your own vain imagination and an oversensitive response on your part? Or, are you upset with them because they remind you so much of yourself?

Step 4

Consciously and deliberately forgive every person who has ever done anything to hurt you.

This step is the most difficult to take. But you must do it. Then, one by one, talk to these Christians. Tell them why you feel as you do. Ask them to forgive you for your attitude—even though they may be primarily at fault.

Remember this word of warning! Don't base your "forgiveness" on the condition that they offer an apology. Take care of your own attitudes and eventually God will take care of theirs.

If a Christian has sinned against you (and others) in such a way that it demands a repentant response, and if you have approached that person in love without receiving a response, then you will need to follow the procedure Jesus outlined in Matthew 18:15-17. Make sure, however, that your approach is characterized by compassion, kindness, humility, gentleness, and patience (Col. 3:12). If it is, chances are you will get a positive response.

Remember too, that we are never justified to take the law into our own hands. Listen to Paul:

> Do not repay anyone evil for evil. Be careful to do what is right in the eyes of everybody. If it is possible, as far as it depends on you, live at peace with everyone. Do not take revenge, my friends, but leave room for God's wrath, for it is written: "It is mine to avenge; I will repay," says the Lord. On the contrary: "If your enemy is hungry, feed him; if he is thirsty, give him something to drink. In doing this, you will

heap burning coals on his head.",Do not be overcome by evil, but overcome evil with good (Rom. 12:17-21).

As a pastor, I had to come to grips with this kind of forgiveness when an arsonist deliberately set fire to our church offices. Over fifty employees were affected. Fifteen of our full-time pastors lost their complete libraries—including yours truly. We were totally wiped out.

This was not just an attack on our church, but an attack on the Gospel and Jesus Christ Himself. As the senior leader in this church, I had to face the issue of forgiveness immediately—and then to lead the whole congregation to forgive the person who had done this terrible thing.

Even today, this arsonist is still at large. Have I forgiven him? Yes! Do I still want justice? Yes! But it's not my responsibility to take the law into my own hands. I'm still praying that he will confess his sin, experience forgiveness, and then turn himself in and pay the penalty for this injustice. In the meantime, I want to "do what is right in the eyes of everybody" (Rom. 12:17).

CORRIE'S STORY

Corrie ten Boom, who suffered incredible persecution in a Nazi concentration camp, is probably one of the most significant modern-day examples of being able to forgive. However, toward the end of her life, she shared that some of her most difficult challenges were to forgive Christian friends. Speaking to this issue she wrote:

I wish I could say after a long and fruitful life traveling the world, I had learned to forgive all my enemies. I wish I could say that merciful and charitable thoughts just naturally flowed from me and on to others. But they don't. There is one thing I've learned since I've passed my eightieth birthday, it's that I can't store up good feelings and behavior—but only draw them fresh from God each day.

Maybe I'm glad it's that way, for every time I go to Him, He teaches me something else. I recall the time—and I was almost seventy—when some Christian friends whom I loved and trusted did something which hurt me. You would have thought that, having been able to forgive the guards in Ravensbruck, forgiving Christian friends would be child's play. It wasn't. For weeks I seethed inside. But at last I asked God again to work His miracle in me. And again it happened: first, the cold-blooded decision, then the flood of joy and peace. I had forgiven my friends; I was restored to my Father.

Then, why was I suddenly awake in the middle of the night, rehashing the whole affair again? My friends! I thought. People I loved. If it had been strangers, I wouldn't have minded so.

I sat up and switched on the light. "Father, I thought it was all forgiven. Please help me do it."

But the next night I woke up again. They'd talked so sweetly too! Never a hint of what they were planning. "Father!" I cried in alarm. "Help me!"

Then it was that another secret of forgiveness became evident. It is not enough to simply say, "I forgive you." I must also begin to live it out. And in my case, that meant acting as though their sins, like mine, were buried in the depths of the deepest sea. If God could remember them no more—and He had said, "[Your] sins and iniquities will I remember no more" (Heb. 10:17)—then neither should I. And the reason the thoughts kept coming back to me was that I kept turning their sin over in my mind.

And so I discovered another of God's principles: We can trust God not only for emotions but also for our thoughts. As I asked Him to renew my mind He also took away my thoughts.

He still had more to teach me, however, even from this single episode. Many years later, after I had passed my eightieth birthday, an American friend came to visit me in Holland. As we sat in my little apartment in Baarn he asked me about those people from long ago who had taken advantage of me.

"It is nothing," I said a little smugly. "It is all forgiven."

"By you, yes," he said. "But what about them? Have they accepted your forgiveness?"

"They say there is nothing to forgive! They deny it ever happened. No matter what they say, though, I can prove they were wrong." I went eagerly to my desk. "See, I have it in black and white! I saved all their letters and I can show you where. . . ."

"Corrie!" My friend slipped his arm through mine and gently closed the drawer. "Aren't you the one whose sins are at the bottom of the sea? Yet are the sins of your friends etched in black and white?"

For an astonishing moment I could not find my voice. "Lord Jesus," I whispered at last, "who takes all my sins away, forgive me for preserving all these years the evidence against others! Give me grace to burn all the blacks and whites as a sweet-smelling sacrifice to Your glory."

I did not go to sleep that night until I had gone through my desk and pulled out those letters—curling now with age—and fed them all into my little coal-burning grate. As the flames leaped and glowed, so did my heart. "Forgive us our trespasses," Jesus taught us to pray, "as we forgive those who trespass against us." In the ashes of those letters I was seeing yet another facet of His mercy. What more He would teach me about forgiveness in the days ahead I didn't know, but tonight's was good news enough.

Forgiveness is the key which unlocks the door of resentment and the handcuffs of hatred. It breaks the chains of bitterness and the shackles of selfishness. The forgiveness of Jesus not only takes away our sins, it makes them as if they had never been.[1]

---

[1] Corrie ten Boom, *Tramp for the Lord*, 181–183. Reprinted by permission.

DISCUSSION GUIDE FOR SMALL GROUPS

OPENING

Have each person share his or her response to these questions:

What is one "pet peeve" you have that annoys you about some-one in your family?

What habit or quirk of your own do you know annoys someone else?

FOR DISCUSSION

1. Can you think of a time when someone showed you consistent patience—perhaps when you were learning a new task or going through a difficult phase in your life? Share it with the group. How did the person's patience affect your relationship with that person? How did it affect your view of yourself? How might your relation-ships be different if you showed that kind of patience to those around you?

2. How easy do you find it to forgive someone who has hurt you—or who has hurt someone you love? What would you say about for-giveness to someone who has suffered abuse?

3. What is the relationship between bearing with one another and admonishing one another or confronting others about their sin? Are our patience and forgiveness affected by the response of the other person? Should they be?

4. If you were to work hard at bearing with one another, what specif-ically would you do? What proactive or preventative action can you take to avoid becoming annoyed with others? What can you do in specific situations when others hurt or annoy you?

CLOSING

Read aloud Matthew 18:21-22 and Colossians 3:13. Allow time for each person, individually and in silence, to write on one sheet of paper all of the offenses others have committed against him or her that are hard to forgive. Then have each person write, on a separate piece of paper, all of the offenses he or she has committed against Christ.

When everyone has finished, place a trash can in the center of the group. Invite group members to offer a prayer of confession (no specifics are necessary) and thanksgiving for God's forgiveness, then crumple and throw away the list of their sins. Then allow each person to pray for the strength to forgive others as they have been forgiven, and discard the list of offenses committed against themselves.

For Next Time

1. Read chapter 11.
2. If you need to take steps to repair a relationship in need of forgiveness, do it this week.

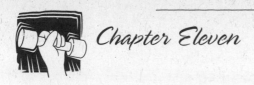 *Chapter Eleven*

Submit to One Another

Submit to one another out of reverence for Christ.

Ephesians 5:21

One day my wife and I were on our way to church. Sitting next to us was our young son, Kenton—then about eight years old. "Are we going to take someone out to dinner after church?" he asked, also mentioning a particular restaurant.

"Yes," I responded. You see, my wife and I had been taking a leadership family out to dinner each Sunday to share our appreciation for their service to the church. We had chosen a rather nice steak house and Kenton had gone along for several Sundays in succession. On that particular day, he responded negatively! "I don't want to go!" he said. "I don't like the food."

My initial reaction was also negative. I wanted to tell him how he should be thankful to be able to go out to eat at all. After all, when I was his age, we couldn't afford to go out to eat—ever. I looked at my wife and I could tell she was thinking the same thing. However, both of us bit our tongues and refrained from saying what we were thinking. Rather than lecturing him on the "blessings of being able to eat out," I asked him where he would like to go.

He responded immediately and mentioned a place where we could order hamburgers and fries. Frankly, that wasn't what we had in mind as a place to take a family for an appreciation dinner. However, once again I held my tongue—and began to ask myself *why* Kenton was reacting.

By the end of the church service, I had sensed I had the answer. As I came off the platform, I shared it with my wife, who had been sitting on the front row. "I think I know why Kenton is reacting," I said. "He's simply bored. By the time we're halfway through the meal—taking time to fellowship together—he's finished, with nothing to do but to sit and wait."

"I know," she said. "I've been thinking the same thing."

"I believe we ought to go where he wants to go!" I responded. Again, Elaine agreed. We also concurred that an eight-year-old boy is far more fond of hamburgers and fries than a steak dinner.

A few minutes later, I saw Kenton walking down the aisle toward the front of the church. I'll never forget the scene. He had his hands in his pockets with a rather sad expression on his face. However, I could also tell he was reconciled to his "father's will"—at least on the outside. What must be, must be!

"Kenton," I called. "Come here a minute."

My son looked up—surprised!

"Yeah, Dad, what do you want?" he said as he approached me.

"Do you still want to go to that hamburger place?" I asked.

Even more surprised, he affirmed his initial request. "Well, then, son," I said, "that's where we're going!"

What happened next surprised me! He threw his arms around me and with deep feeling said. "Oh, Dad, I love you!"

That day we went to that little fast food place. In fact, it turned out to be the best place for the family who came along since they had two small children. Incidentally, it turned out to be a lot less expensive too.

But what happened that day during the meal taught both my wife and me an even greater lesson. Kenton positioned himself between these two children, put one arm around one of them and then the other—and "fathered" them through the whole meal. It didn't take long for my wife and me to see what was happening. Our eight-year-old son was expressing his appreciation to us for going where he wanted to go. In fact, he was actually caring for these two children by keeping them occupied so we could visit with their parents. Needless to say, I was deeply touched. As parents, we had "submitted" to our young son—and he was responding with love and appreciation.

Did we lose Kenton's respect that day? No, we won his respect. Did he try to take advantage of us the next time? No, he was even more cooperative. In fact, a week or so later, we were driving along in the car and suddenly, out of the blue, he said, "Dad, sometimes I think you allow me to do too many things I want to do!"

Surprised, I could see what had happened. Kenton was still feeling guilty that we had submitted to his desires. "No, son," I said. "You don't take advantage of us! I'm glad at times we can do what you want to do—even though it may not be our first choice."

Kenton is now a grown man, but he has never forgotten that incident—the day his parents submitted to him. And I've never forgotten it either. And I also learned a very important principle that applies to many different kinds of relationships. Even though we may be in a position of authority, submitting to others who report to us does not undermine our position. In fact, when it's appropriate, we'll win respect for who we are and the position we hold. Certainly, there will be a few people who will take advantage of the situation. But when they do, they're very immature people—much more immature than my eight-year-old son.

A BIBLICAL PERSPECTIVE

The concept of "submission" is used by biblical writers to describe a variety of Christian relationships. Paul exhorted all Christians (both men and women) to "submit to one another" (Eph. 5:21). Peter exhorted young men to "be submissive to those who are older" (1 Peter 5:5). All members of Christ's body are exhorted to "obey" their "leaders and submit to their authority" (Heb. 13:17). Servants are instructed to submit to their masters (Titus 2:9; Eph. 6:5; Col. 3:22; 1 Peter 2:18)—which applies when serving either

Christian or non-Christian masters. Children are admonished to obey and submit to their parents (Eph. 6:1; Col. 3:20). Furthermore, Christians are also instructed to submit to other authority figures in their lives who are not Christians—particularly those who are leaders in government (Rom. 13:1; 1 Peter 2:13).

Servant Leadership

The Bible makes it clear that Christians who are in positions of authority must also function with a submissive attitude. Husbands are directed to love their wives "just as Christ loved the church" (Eph. 5:25). We cannot love like Christ without being servants, and we cannot be servants without being submissive. This may sound paradoxical but this is what Christ did for us when He became flesh and dwelt among us!

Fathers are to deal sensitively with their children, understanding and meeting their needs (Eph. 6:4; Col. 3:21). This we cannot do without serving them.

Elders or pastors are commissioned to be "servants." As leaders, we are to be "eager to serve" (1 Peter 5:2). We are not to lord it over other Christians, using our position as a means of unjust gain—either financially, psychologically, or socially (1 Peter 5:1-4).

Christian masters are to treat their servants fairly and sensitively just as Christ treated us when He gave Himself for us (Eph. 6:9; Col. 4:1). In Christ, these people were not only slaves but brothers in Christ. When they were treated this way, the slavery system in the New Testament church eventually disappeared. Slave holders saw that this social disease was incompatible with Christianity. It is interesting that Paul didn't attack slavery per se but actually destroyed it by teaching masters to love their slaves as Christ loved them. Not surprisingly, this approach also changed women's marital status in the Roman world—both among Gentiles and Jews. How could a Christian husband treat his wife as inferior when he believed she was his spiritual equal in Christ (Gal. 3:28). This also demonstrates it is possible to maintain our position of authority, both in the family and in the church, and yet be a servant.

Mutual Submission

When Jesus Christ was on earth, He said to His disciples one day when they were arguing among themselves regarding who was to be the greatest in His kingdom:

> You know that the rulers of the Gentiles lord it over them, and their high officials exercise authority over them. Not so with you. Instead, whoever wants to become great among you must be your servant, and whoever wants to be first must be your slave—just as the Son of Man did not come to be served, but to serve, and to give His life a ransom for many (Matt. 20:25-28).

Being able to submit to one another no matter what our position of authority is a distinct concept made possible by Jesus Christ. Christianity is unique. When Christ came into this world, He brought into being a whole new approach to functional relationships between people. In the "Gentile world," as Jesus called it, there was no such thing as mutual submission. Even acts of obedience and submission became a means to selfish ends. But, in Christ, all believers have the potential to "submit to one another out of reverence for Christ."

CHRIST'S EXAMPLE

This is what Jesus Christ demonstrated for us, when He, the Lord of the universe, became a servant to all men. He, "who, being in very nature God, did not consider equality with God something to be grasped, but made himself nothing" (Phil. 2:6-7). Paul made it clear that all Christians—even those in authority—are to follow Christ's example. We are to love as Christ loved. We are to "do nothing out of selfish ambition or vain conceit, but in humility consider others better than ourselves." We are to "look not only to [our] own interests, but also to the interests of others" (Phil. 2:3-4). We are to "submit to one another out of reverence for Christ" (Eph. 5:21)—the One who set the perfect example. Our attitude "should be the same as that of Christ Jesus" (Phil. 2:5).

Selfishness

Unfortunately, not all Christians in positions of authority have the mind of Christ. Some men use the concept of submission and headship to lord it over their wives and others, to force them into subservient roles. In reality, they have used the Bible as a "club"—a means to get their own way. This is not "loving as Christ loved." It's selfishness. When we do this, we have not learned that we cannot earn respect by demanding it. For it to be real and meaningful, it must be earned.

Insecurity

I remember one incident when I was just a young husband. I made it clear that we were going to do it my way—and we did! Later, I had to admit that my wife's idea was far better. I also had to admit that I made my decision not out of love but because I wanted to defend my position as head of the household. As a young husband, I wanted to establish myself as the leader. Though my wife knew better—and was hurt in the process—she willing submitted. Unfortunately, I didn't win much respect that day. I later had to ask forgiveness. To my wife's credit, she accepted my apology, forgave me—and never brought the issue up again. In that sense, she handled it far more maturely than I did.

Confusion

Some Christian men are also confused regarding what the Bible teaches. I was talking with a husband one day whose wife had left him. "Why did she leave?" I asked. "My wife thinks I try to control her," he responded.

"Do you?" I asked in turn.

"Well, the Bible tells me I am supposed to 'rule over' her," he said, quoting Genesis 3:16.

Trying to be sensitive to this very misguided response, I pointed out to him that he had totally misinterpreted what God had said. "That's the result of sin," I replied. "When Adam and Eve sinned, she—and all of her female children and great-great-grandchildren—will be tempted to usurp their husband's authority. But as husbands," I continued, "our temptation will be to dominate, control, and abuse our wives." Believe it or not, this young man was totally surprised. He had not only misinterpreted Scripture, but he had rationalized his sin.

Fortunately, when Jesus Christ came and provided salvation and sent the Holy Spirit to dwell within us, we can experience a wonderful restoration in our lives as husbands and wives, as parents and children, as pastors and people, and as brothers and sisters in Jesus Christ. We can carry out our God-ordained roles as leaders and, at the same time, be servants to one another. This, of course, involves submission in certain instances. Furthermore, as followers, we can submit to those who are in authority without attempting to manipulate and resist. In other words, we can "submit to one another out of reverence for Christ."

BIBLICAL GUIDELINES

Paul made it very clear that submission to other Christians should not be based on subjective impulses and reactions. If they are, we can be responding selfishly. Rather, the guidelines for mutual submission are rooted in the authority of Jesus Christ and His Word. Thus, in a parallel passage, Paul exhorted the Colossians:

> Let the *word of Christ* dwell in you richly as you teach and admonish one another with all wisdom, and as you sing psalms, hymns and spiritual songs with gratitude in your hearts to God. And whatever you do, whether in word or deed, do it all in the name of the Lord Jesus (Col. 3:16-17).

No Christian has the right to request something of another Christian that is not based in the Word of God. When we are asked to violate the will of God, we must obey God rather than men (Acts 4:19; 5:29). However, when we resist because we're being asked to do something that is wrong, we must do so with respect. Oftentimes, God honors our attitude and softens the heart of the person who is trying to violate us in our relationship with Jesus Christ.

There are Christians, however, who are in authority who will continue to put pressure on others to violate the will of God. When this happens, we must understand that we can appeal to a higher authority in the church—namely, our spiritual leaders. This applies to wives whose husbands are abusive or unethical or immoral. If husbands do not respond to loving exhortations from their spouses, the offended parties (their wives) have the right to seek help from their spiritual leaders, following the procedure outlined by Jesus Christ (Matt. 18:15-17). In this sense, a wife must be viewed as a "sister in Christ" as well as a spouse. She has biblical rights and values that should not be violated by her husband—also her "brother in Christ." Then, if she is being subjective and rationalizing her own lack of submission, this too will be discovered by mature spiritual leaders in the church who can sensitively exhort and guide her in her relationship with her husband.

PRACTICAL STEPS FOR MUTUAL SUBMISSION

The following steps are designed to help all Christians submit to one another.

Step 1

Mutual submission must begin with the leadership of the church.

What Paul was teaching must be modeled before all other members of the local body. If there is contention and lack of harmony in the pastoral staff and among elders and deacons, it will become obvious to all other members of the local Christian family. Just as tension between a husband and wife cannot be hidden from children, so lack of oneness among leaders of a church cannot be hidden from the rest of the congregation.

The converse is also true. A group of leaders who are truly one in Christ becomes a dynamic example for those for whom they are responsible. The love and unity they experience and demonstrate at the leadership level will filter through the whole church.

HE THAT IS GREATEST IS TO BE SERVANT OF ALL

I serve as senior pastor of Fellowship Bible Church North in Plano, Texas. I am also an elder and serve with seven other godly men. Though I also serve as chairman of the board, I have purposely put myself under the other men's authority. I have made myself accountable to them for my actions.

But at the same time, I also serve with these men as equals. When we make decisions, I work hard at not overriding these men's opinions with my own. I serve *with them* at this level of leadership. We are fellow pastors.

However, these men also look to me as their leader. They respect my opinions and listen carefully to my recommendations. They definitely recognize me as their senior leader.

With this arrangement, I operate at three levels. First, I'm accountable to these men—by choice. Second, I work with them as equals in decision making. Third, I'm their leader. This structure I believe is in harmony with what Jesus taught His disciples when He said, "If anyone wants to be first, he must be the very last, and the servant of all" (Mark 9:35). Jesus, who was God in human flesh, also modeled this leadership style to the apostles when He as their "Lord and Teacher" washed their feet (John 13:14).

To make this plan work effectively, a great deal depends on my own attitude—and theirs as well. At this point, our motives and our methods must blend in beautiful harmony. Keep in mind that no pattern or structure will work effectively if we violate the principles and teachings of the Word of God.

Step 2

All believers must clearly understand the teaching of Scripture regarding the subject of submission.

This is not only a directive for wives, children, and employees— but for all members of Christ's body. We must realize that it is possible for husbands to submit to their wives without giving up their headship; for elders to submit to others in Christ's body without giving up their position of authority; that parents can listen to the children's viewpoint without giving up parental status; for employers to give employees careful consideration without losing respect. The key is for all Christians to develop the mind of Christ, to be willing to lose their lives in order to find them again.

Step 3

Meditate on the following Scriptures that teach submission and obedience to others.

Note the variety of relationships in the context of each directive. Use these Scriptures as a criteria for evaluating your own attitude toward other members of Christ's body. *Circle* the areas where you feel you are strong. *Underscore* the areas where you feel you need to improve.

Elders to Other Members of Christ's Body

Be shepherds of God's flock that is under your care, serving as overseers—not because you must, but because you are willing, as God wants you to be; not greedy for money, but eager to serve; not lording it over those entrusted to you, but being examples to the flock (1 Peter 5:2-3).

Christians in General to Elders

The elders who direct the affairs of the church well are worthy of double honor, especially those whose work is preaching and teaching (1 Tim. 5:17).

Obey your leaders and submit to their authority. They keep watch over you as men who must give an account. Obey them so that their work will be a joy, not a burden, for that would be of no advantage to you (Heb. 13:17).

Younger Men to Older Men

Young men, in the same way be submissive to those who are older. . . . Clothe yourselves with humility toward one another, because, "God opposes the proud but gives grace to the humble." Humble yourselves, therefore, under God's mighty hand, that he may lift you up in due time (1 Peter 5:5-6).

Husbands to Wives

Husbands, love your wives, just as Christ loved the church and gave himself up for her. . . . Husbands ought to love their wives as their own bodies. He who loves his wife loves himself (Eph. 5:25, 28).

Husbands, love your wives and do not be harsh with them (Col. 3:19).

Husbands, in the same way be considerate as you live with your wives, and treat them with respect as the weaker partner and as heirs with you of the gracious gift of life, so that nothing will hinder your prayers (1 Peter 3:7).

The husband should fulfill his marital duty to his wife, and likewise the wife to her husband. A wife's body does not belong to her alone but also to her husband. In the same way, a husband's body does not belong to him alone but also to his wife (1 Cor. 7:3-4).

Wives to Their Husbands

Wives, submit to your husbands as to the Lord. . . . Now as the church submits to Christ, so also wives should submit to their husbands in everything (Eph. 5:22-24).

Wives, submit to your husbands, as is fitting in the Lord (Col. 3:18).

Likewise, teach the older women to be reverent in the way they live, not to be slanderers or addicted to much wine, but to teach what is good. Then they can train the younger women to love their husbands and children, to be self-controlled and pure, to be busy at home, to be kind, and to be subject to their husbands, so that no one will malign the word of God (Titus 2:3-5).

Wives, in the same way be submissive to your husbands so that, if any of them do not believe the word, they may be won over without words by the behavior of their wives, when they see the purity and reverence of your lives. Your beauty should not come from outward adornment, such as braided hair and the wearing of gold jewelry and fine clothes. Instead, it should be that of your inner self, the unfading beauty of a gentle and quiet spirit, which is of great worth in God's sight (1 Peter 3:1-4).

Parents to Children

Fathers, do not exasperate your children; instead, bring them up in the training and instruction of the Lord (Eph. 6:4).

Fathers, do not embitter your children, or they will become discouraged (Col. 3:21).

Children to Parents

Children, obey your parents in the Lord, for this is right. "Honor your father and mother"—which is the first commandment with a promise—"that it may go well with you and that you may enjoy long life on the earth" (Eph. 6:1-3).

Children, obey your parents in everything, for this pleases the Lord (Col. 3:20).

Masters (Employers) to Servants (Employees)

And masters, treat your slaves the same way. Do not threaten them, since you know that he who is both their Master and yours is in heaven, and there is no favoritism with him (Eph. 6:9).

Masters, provide your slaves with what is right and fair, because you know that you also have a Master in heaven (Col. 4:1).

Servants (Employees) to Masters (Employers)

Slaves, obey your earthly masters with respect and fear, and with sincerity of heart, just as you would obey Christ. Obey them not only to win their favor when their eye is on you, but like slaves of Christ, doing the will of God from your heart. Serve wholeheartedly, as if you were serving the Lord, not men, because you know that the Lord will reward everyone for whatever good he does, whether he is slave or free (Eph. 6:5-8; see also Col. 3:22-25).

Slaves, submit yourselves to your masters with all respect, not only to those who are good and considerate, but also to those who are harsh (1 Peter 2:18).

Christians to Government Officials

Everyone must submit himself to the governing authorities, for there is no authority except that which God has established. . . . Therefore, it is necessary to submit to the authorities, not only because of possible punishment but also because of conscience. . . . Give everyone what you owe him: If you owe taxes, pay taxes, if revenue, then revenue; if respect, then respect; if honor, then honor (Rom. 13:1, 5, 7).

Submit yourselves for the Lord's sake to every authority instituted among men: whether to the king, as the supreme authority, or to governors, who are sent by him to punish those who do wrong and to commend those who do right. For it is God's will that by doing good you should silence the ignorant talk of foolish men. Live as free men, but do not use your freedom as a cover-up for evil; live as servants of God. Show proper respect to everyone: Love the brotherhood of believers, fear God, honor the king (1 Peter 2:13-17).

Step 4

Evaluate and prioritize the areas where you need to improve.

Now that you have isolated your strengths and weaknesses, go back and number the areas where you need improvement. Give yourself a number one in the area of greatest need; a number two in the next area, etc.

Step 5

Set some specific goals.

To begin, select the area where you need the most improvement. Set up one specific goal and an action step you are going to take to become more obedient to Jesus Christ in this area. Select one new area each week and set a new goal until you have covered them all.

Keep reviewing and remind yourself of your previous goals. Pray continually that God will help you obey His Word in these areas.

DISCUSSION GUIDE FOR SMALL GROUPS

OPENING

Share your responses to the following questions:

What is your emotional reaction to being told to submit to someone else?

What is your emotional reaction to hearing that someone must submit to you?

FOR DISCUSSION

1. Why is the topic of submission often such an emotionally thorny topic? How has the concept of submission been abused in the church? In society? What is the difference between the biblical view of submission and society's view?

2. In what ways did Jesus model submission? How does His example shape your perspective of what it means to submit? How does it affect your personal attitude toward being a submissive person?

3. In what circumstances, if any, can a person call for others to submit to him or her? In what circumstances should a person urge others to submit to someone else? What should you do if the person to whom you are called to submit abuses that authority?

4. Divide into smaller groups according to the categories in Step 3 of "Practical Steps"—elders in one subgroup, young men in another, wives in another, and so on. Let those who fit into more than one subgroup choose the one that most interests them. In subgroups, read the Scripture passages listed and discuss specifically what that kind of submission would look like in your life in the next week or month.

CLOSING

Still in subgroups, set up a simple means of supporting and holding one another accountable (for example, each person might have a partner to call during the week), and pray for one another.

For Next Time

1. Read chapter 12.
2. Act on your personal goal.
3. Follow through on the support and accountability plan your sub-group developed.

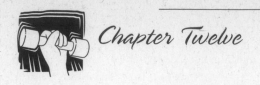

Chapter Twelve

Encouraging One Another

> Therefore encourage one another and build each
> other up.
>
> *1 Thessalonians 5:11*

A number of years ago, I learned a very powerful lesson. I was serving as director of the Moody Evening School in Chicago—a ministry to laypeople. About a thousand students attended. Most of these people held full-time jobs, but served as Sunday School teachers, board members, deacons, elders—and in other lay positions in their churches. Some simply came to Moody Bible Institute to increase their knowledge of the Bible.

As director of this school, I used to speak in various churches throughout the Chicago area and the suburbs in order to let people know about our ministry and how we could serve them.

On one occasion, a woman introduced herself after I had spoken at a Sunday evening service. She wanted me to know what a blessing Dr. Charles Horn was in her life. Chuck was one of our professors. "I never miss that class he is teaching on the Book of Romans," she said. "During the day I work as a secretary in downtown Chicago," she continued, "and I am always tired when I get to school. However, that course is changing my life!"

I remember jotting down what she had said and the next morning when I arrived in my office, I called this professor on the telephone. Frankly, I simply relayed to him what this woman had told me. As I did, I could "hear" the silence on the other end of the phone. And then I heard the following words encased in a context of deep sincerity and appreciation, "Thank you. Thank you very much, Gene! I needed that!"

"Well," I said, "this student really appreciates you, Chuck. Your ministry is changing her life. And I appreciate you too! Thanks for your faithfulness."

Little did I realize then that my telephone call that morning was life changing for this professor. Subsequently, I discovered that in all of his years of teaching this was the first time that he had ever received positive feedback from one of his superiors. "This should never happen—not among Christians!" I remember thinking to myself.

FAITHFULNESS SHOULD BE REWARDED

Chuck was a faithful teacher. He is now in heaven, but it has never been God's plan for His servants to have to wait to receive their rewards till they are rewarded in heaven. That's why He has instructed us to "honor one another." Mutual encouragement is definitely a dual concept!

Because of this experience, I set a new goal—to encourage the other professors with positive verbal feedback. Consequently, I tuned my ears to what students were saying and made it a point to ask questions that generated this kind of information. I then looked for natural opportunities to pass this information on to the other professors.

When I took over this ministry, I knew that faculty morale was at an all-time low, simply because no one had occupied this position for several years. Consequently, the teachers—most who also taught in the day school—had come to view this ministry as an obligation rather than an opportunity. However, one day after I had begun this new approach to encouragement, I received a call from the director of personnel. "Gene," he said, "I don't know what you're doing, but I've never seen such a positive change in a group of employees."

"It's simple, John," I replied. "I just listen for positive comments from the students and pass them on to the professors!"

A NEGLECTED EXHORTATION

Why are we so hesitant to encourage others? Why do we neglect this very important biblical responsibility? In fact, some Christians seem to feel they possess the "gift of discouragement." The only time they communicate anything to others is when they have something negative to say! Either that, or they say nothing at all—which can be just as discouraging.

To be fair, some of this neglect is based on the misunderstanding that successful public figures don't need positive feedback. The facts are, all Christians need it! On occasion, people come up to me after a service when they have been deeply touched by a message or series of messages and say, "Gene, I'm sure you hear this all the time, but"—and then they go on to share their appreciation. I want to respond by saying—"No, people don't say that kind of thing all the time! However, I wish they did!"

You see, many people just don't believe that leaders who appear to have it all together need encouragement. But we all do, and the truth is that no matter how successful we are, none of us "has it together" as well as it may appear when we are on the platform delivering a message or in front of a classroom giving a lecture. Even when we do a great job in ministry, we need positive feedback to keep on keeping on for Jesus! We all tend at times to second-guess our effectiveness. We all need encouragement!

"ANOTHER PARAKLETOS"

Following Christ's return to heaven, God's plan for continuing what His Son had done focused on the Holy Spirit. Four times in John's Gospel, Jesus identified the Holy Spirit as a "counselor" (John 14:16, 26; 15:26; 16:7). Translators of the *King James Version* call Him "another Comforter." In the *New American Standard Bible*, He is identified as "another *Helper*."

Why these different English titles? The word in the language of the Greek New Testament is *parakletos,* and it's transliterated into English as "another *paraclete*." The important correlation here is that the Greek verb *parakaleo* is frequently translated "to encourage." Therefore, it would also be appropriate to identify the Holy Spirit in this passage as "another *encourager*"—which is why the *King James Version* uses the synonym "comforter."

At this time in their lives, the apostles were very fearful. Their hearts were "troubled" (John 14:27). Hatred toward them by the religious leaders in Jerusalem had never been more intense. It was no secret that there had been several attempts to kill their leader. This was why Jesus "no longer moved about publicly" (11:54). No wonder these men were frightened and discouraged when Jesus announced His plans to leave them!

In actuality, Jesus was not going to leave them. He would still be present in the person of the Holy Spirit. This is why He said, "The world cannot accept him [as counselor], because it neither sees him nor knows him. But *you know him, for he lives with you and will be in you*" (14:17). With this statement, Jesus introduced them to the Holy Spirit. Though the Spirit is a separate person in the Godhead, yet He is one with the Father and the Son. He who has seen the Son has seen the Father; likewise, he who had seen the Son had also seen a manifestation of the Holy Spirit. They are three persons, yet one God. And while Jesus was on earth, He revealed the Father and the Spirit.

The Holy Spirit was then to be "another Counselor"—another *encourager*. He would continue Christ's work on earth. He would never leave the apostles—or others who followed Christ.

Though the eleven apostles did not yet understand all of Jesus' statements about the Holy Spirit, they were soon to find out what He meant. Following Christ's death, resurrection, and ascension, they and a small band of believers waited in Jerusalem as Jesus had told them to (Luke 24:49). And while there, the Holy Spirit came as Jesus had promised. It was a dramatic event. He gifted some of them so they would be able to recall, understand, and communicate. God's truth. He empowered some of them to work miracles in order to verify the message they were teaching.

Jesus also identified the Holy Spirit as "*the Spirit of truth*." He did this three times while encouraging the apostles in their time of stress and difficulty:

> And I will ask the Father, and he will give you another Counselor [*encourager*] to be with you forever—*the Spirit of Truth* (John 14:16-17).

> When the Counselor [*encourager*] comes, whom I will send to you from the Father, the Spirit of truth who goes out from the Father, he will testify about me (15:26).

> I have much more to say to you, more than you can now bear. But when he, the Spirit of Truth, comes, he will guide you into all truth. He will not speak on his own; he will speak only what he hears, and he will tell you what is yet to come (John 16:12-13).

THE INSPIRED WORD OF GOD

When the Holy Spirit came, He fulfilled Jesus' promise. One of His greatest gifts to us is the inspired Scriptures. The authors of the inscripted Word "spoke from God as they were carried along by the Holy Spirit" (2 Peter 1:21) and Paul told Timothy that "all Scripture is God-breathed" (2 Tim. 3:16). He was definitely referring to the ministry of the Holy Spirit as He inspired those who penned the Word of God.

The primary means then for "encouraging one another" is God's truth! This is why Paul wrote to the Ephesian Christians, encouraging them to continue "speaking the *truth* in love." Then, he said, "We will in all things grow up into him who is the Head, that is, Christ" (Eph. 4:15).

There are many biblical examples that demonstrate that the basis for encouraging other believers is the Word of God. For example, when Paul outlined the qualities for eldership in his Letter to Titus, he emphasized that a pastoral leader "must hold firmly to the *trustworthy* message as it has been taught, so that he can *encourage others by sound doctrine*" (Titus 1:9).

When Paul wrote to Timothy, he charged this young pastor to "*preach the Word.*" He was to "be prepared in season and out of season" in order to "*correct, rebuke* and *encourage*" (2 Tim. 4:2). Furthermore, when Paul, Silas, and Timothy discipled the new Christians at Thessalonica, they dealt with each one of these people just as a "father deals with his own children, *encouraging, comforting,* and *urging* [them] to live lives worthy of God" (1 Thes. 2:11-12). Paul then went on immediately to describe the means for this encouragement when he wrote:

> We also thank God continually because, when you received the word of God, which you heard from us, you accepted it not as the word of men, but as it actually is, the word of God, which is at work in you who believe (1 Thes. 2:13).

A KEY TO SPIRITUAL GROWTH

The most comprehensive New Testament passage instructing us to encourage one another appears in the Letter to the Hebrews. The specific injunction reads—

> Let us not give up meeting together, as some are in the habit of doing, but let us encourage one another—and all the more as you see the Day approaching (Heb. 10:25).[1]

What should happen to Christians when they meet together regularly and "encourage one another"? First, we should *grow in our faith* (Heb. 10:22). Second, we should *grow in our hope* (Heb.

---

[1]Though the specific word *allelon*, which is translated "one another," is not used in the original text in Hebrews 10:25, it is used in Hebrews 10:24. The idea in verse 25 is an extension of this concept. Therefore, the translators are very much in order to use the words "one another" in verse 25.

10:23). Third, we should *grow in our love* (Heb. 10:24).

More than any other quality, mutual encouragement among members of the body of Christ should "spur one another on towards *love* and good deeds" (v. 24). Paul underscored this truth when writing to the Corinthians. Summarizing at the end of that great passage in 1 Corinthians, he said, "And now these three remain: *faith, hope,* and *love.* But the greatest of these is love" (1 Cor. 13:13).

A MESSAGE OF ENCOURAGEMENT

Though the Thessalonian Christians understood that Jesus Christ was going to return to take them to heaven, they did not really know what would happen to Christians who died *before* Christ returned. Evidently, some of their Christian friends had already passed away since Paul's initial ministry in Thessalonica and they were very concerned about their loved ones' eternal destiny. This may seem like a very elementary question for us, but it was a very profound question for these believers who had been converted out of raw paganism.

Paul dealt with this question in his first letter. "We do not want you to be ignorant about those who fall asleep [that is, those who have died]," Paul wrote, "or to grieve like the rest of men, who have no hope" (1 Thes. 4:13). Then Paul gave the reason they should not grieve: "We believe that Jesus died and rose again and so we believe that God will bring with Jesus those who have fallen asleep in him" (v. 14).

Paul made it clear that all believers—dead or alive—will be part of the Rapture. "The dead in Christ will rise first," he reassured them, and then "after that, we who are still alive and are left will be caught up together with them in the clouds to meet the Lord in the air" (4:17). To make sure they understood this matter clearly, he stated: "And so we will be with the Lord forever" (v. 17).

I often use this passage of Scripture when I speak at funerals. The reason is obvious. Paul told us to "*encourage each other* with these words" (1 Thes. 4:18; see also 5:11). Paul was not denying that there would be sorrow when loved ones die. Rather, he told them that their grief was different. Their separation was only temporary. They would be united again when Jesus Christ comes to take all His children home to heaven—those who have died and those who are still alive.

THE POWER OF WORDS

The focus of Paul's exhortations to "encourage one another" in the Thessalonian epistle is on "words of truth" that come directly from the Bible regarding the second coming of Jesus Christ. But in addition to correct doctrine, there are many other "word" messages we can use to encourage one another. When we use them appropriately, they have a profound impact on those who hear them. For example, consider the following proverb:

An anxious heart weighs a man down, but a kind word cheers him up (Prov. 12:25).

This is what I did for my friend Chuck in the Moody Evening School. In many respects, he had a heavy heart—simply because he felt discouraged. He wasn't sure if anyone really appreciated what he was doing. Consequently, when I offered "a kind word," it cheered him up. It made him feel good about himself.

At times, all of us have experienced the kind of anxiety spoken about in this proverb. It's a heavy feeling that comes over us when we are troubled about something. It may be caused by family illness or the death of a close friend or loved one. For one or many reasons, we may be disappointed in ourselves. We have inadvertently hurt someone's feelings or let someone down. We may have failed to achieve some goal that was important to us. Or we may be disappointed in someone else who has let us down. In this proverb, Solomon is simply telling us that we can counter the effects of a heavy heart with a kind word. In fact, we can change a person's whole perspective on life. It's so simple. It costs nothing. Why don't we do it more often? Unfortunately, we're too often so wrapped up in our own world we don't think about others.

> Pleasant words are a honeycomb, sweet to the soul and healing to the bones (Prov. 16:24).

This second proverb treats another important dimension of encouragement. This time, Solomon wrote about *pleasant words* that are like honey. They're "sweet to the *soul* and healing to the *bones*."

Man is basically a two-dimensional creature—both soul/spirit and body. To put it another way, we are both psychological beings and physical beings and, of course, both are interrelated, so much so that we often talk about experiencing "psychosomatic" conditions. The first part of this word, "psycho" comes from the Greek word *psuche*, meaning "soul." The second part of the word, "somatic," comes from the Greek word *soma* meaning "body." Therefore, "psychosomatic" refers to both the "soul" and "body." Pleasant words affect both our psychological and physical being in a positive way.

On the other hand, Solomon also reminds us that the opposite is true. He also penned this proverb—"A cheerful heart is good medicine, but *a crushed spirit dries up the bones*" (Prov. 17:22). Are you a "healer" or a "hurter"? An important means to help people feel good all over is to use *pleasant words*.

> A word aptly spoken is like apples of gold in settings of silver (Prov. 25:11).

There's an event in my childhood that I will never forget. I was only six years old and in the first grade. My teacher, whose name was Miss Olive Owens, went to the chalkboard and wrote the word "me" in what I know now was cursive. She then told all of us to copy this word on our tablets.

You must understand I had never seen the word "me"—either written or printed. These were pre-"Sesame Street" days, and try as I might, I couldn't get my pencil to cooperate.

Miss Owens then began to walk down each aisle, looking at each student's effort. I was in the third row—about three-quarters of the way back from the front of the room. She made her way down the first aisle, then up the second—and then started down my aisle. I was gripped with fear and my heart began to pound! What my hand had produced on my paper looked like the scribblings of a runaway seismograph!

But the traumatic moment came! Miss Owens stopped at my desk. My anxiety and tension was too much for me to handle. Tears filled my eyes as I lowered my head in shame. You see, I loved my teacher and I didn't want to fail her. Furthermore, I was afraid I would be publicly reprimanded.

Miss Owens immediately sensed the cause of my anxiety. I'll *never* forget what happened next. I can almost feel the emotional relief as I pen these words. She leaned over and quietly whispered in my ear so no one else could hear. "That's all right, Gene," she said as she bent over and kissed me gently on the cheek and went on to the next desk!

Do you understand why I'll never forget that moment? What if she had scolded me, and told me to straighten up and "act like a big boy"! I would have been devastated. I was already embarrassed—and perhaps that would have been the beginning of a deep resentment toward my teacher and my school. Rather, from that moment forward, I was proud to be her student. I looked forward to school. And I worked hard to please my teacher.

There is an interesting sequel to this story. Years later when I was in college, I heard that Miss Owens had died of cancer. Though I was over a thousand miles away, I literally felt pain in my chest. Part of me seemed to feel what she had suffered. There is no question that what I was experiencing at that moment can be traced back to that day in the first grade when she encouraged me with some very kind words that were spoken at just the right moment and in the right context. This I believe is a powerful example of what this proverb means: "A word aptly spoken is like apples of gold in settings of silver" (Prov. 25:11).

"BARNABAS—SON OF ENCOURAGEMENT"

The Lord has given us a dynamic New Testament example of a man who encouraged others—and *why* he was such an encourager. His name was Joseph, but the apostles changed it to Barnabas—which means "son of encouragement."

We first meet Barnabas in the midst of an economic crisis. He demonstrated unusual generosity in helping care for needy believers in Jerusalem. He was a capable businessman from Cyprus who had invested wisely in real estate in Jerusalem and the surrounding area. Seeing the need to help the apostles meet the physical needs of those new Christians who had decided to stay in Jerusalem, he voluntarily sold "a field he owned" and gave the entire proceeds to the apostles to distribute among these new converts.

A Generous Man

Why did the Holy Spirit inspire Luke to record this event so we could read about it nearly two thousands years later? First, the Lord wants us to be exposed to His *example of generosity*. Second, the Lord wants all of us to know that *generous people are real encouragers*. Ask any pastor or Christian leader what encourages them the most in carrying out God's work! Invariably, they will respond by stating that Christians who generously support the ministry with their monetary gifts remove a great burden from their shoulders—which is why these people are a great source of encouragement.

A People Person

But Barnabas was also an "encourager" because of his devotion to people. When Paul returned to Jerusalem—approximately three years following his conversion (Gal. 1:18)—he was still greatly suspect. Luke recorded that "he tried to join the disciples, but they were *all afraid of him, not believing that he really was a disciple*" (Acts 9:26). They were convinced he was feigning his conversion in order to get "inside the system"—and then at the right moment to strike out as he had done before! Though several years had gone by, they had not forgotten how this man had orchestrated Stephen's death and introduced an all-out attack against the church (8:1-3).

But Barnabas had developed a deep relationship with Paul. He knew this former persecutor was for real. He had the courage to go directly to the "top"—to the apostles—in order to intervene for his friend (9:27).

Any time you believe in someone, you are taking a risk. Barnabas was willing to take that risk—but not on blind faith. He had taken time to get the facts about Paul—to discover the truth. First, he told the apostles that Paul "had seen the Lord." Second, he knew that "the Lord spoke" directly to Paul. Third, he had heard him preach "fearlessly in the name of Jesus" while in Damascus (9:27). Barnabas also knew that Paul had to flee for his own life because of his bold stand for the Gospel (9:23-25).

Encouragers give people the benefit of the doubt. Even when other people are skeptical or simply refuse to get involved in helping someone who needs a character reference, encouragers take time to get the facts—just like Barnabas—and then "step up to the plate" and "go to bat" for that person.

An Impartial Christian

There is another very important reason why Barnabas was such an encourager. He was *free from prejudice*. Following the intense persecution in Jerusalem, a number of Jewish believers "traveled as far as Phoenicia, Cyprus and Antioch, *telling the message only to Jews*" (11:19). Even the apostles still believed the Gospel was a message for Jews only. But Luke recorded that "men from Cyprus and Cyrene [Grecian Jews like Barnabas] . . . began to speak to Greeks also, telling them the good news about the Lord Jesus" (11:20). Consequently, many of these Gentiles believed in the Gospel and were saved.

This was a great surprise to the Jewish Christians who lived in Jerusalem. Struggling with deep prejudice in their hearts—even as Christians—they concluded that they had no choice but to respond to what was happening. But who would go? Who would be *willing* to go? Finally, they decided to send Barnabas to Antioch in order to encourage these people in their faith (11:22).

The message is clear. Barnabas was a fair-minded man. He had lived among the Gentiles for years. He did business with them. He had eaten with them. He knew they were God's creation just like himself. He was "a good man, full of the Holy Spirit"—the one Jesus identified as the *parakletos* (an encourager) (Acts 11:24). When he arrived in Antioch and "saw the evidence of the grace of

God" in these Gentiles' lives, "*he was glad and encouraged them* all to remain true to the Lord with all their hearts" (11:23).

Only people who are free from prejudice can get truly excited about the good things that happen to people who are different from them. This is another reason that Joseph's name was changed to Barnabas—"son of encouragement." He was an impartial Christian.

Are You an Encourager Like Barnabas?

The following questions will help you do a reality check in your own life:

Are you a generous Christian?

What percentage of your income do you actually give to the Lord's work on a regular basis?

Are you a trusting Christian? Do you believe in people, seeing the best in them? Do you take time to really get to know people?

Are you an accepting Christian? Do you accept others as Christ accepted you? (Rom. 15:7) More specifically, are you free from prejudice? Or do you believe that you are better than other people because of your ethnic or religious background?

PRACTICAL STEPS FOR ENCOURAGING ONE ANOTHER

Step 1

Learn to use the Word of God.

All Christians must realize how important the Word of God is in building up others within the body of Christ. And all Christians must be challenged to learn what God's Word says. They must be ready to share the Word with others who are in special need of encouragement. In other words, Christians cannot mutually encourage one another with Scripture if they are not familiar with Scripture. Therefore, encourage each believer in your church to study the Word of God—not only for personal growth, but to be able to assist others in their growth.

Step 2

Allow the Holy Spirit to minister through all members of the body.

I noticed a man walk into a "small group" one day who had not been present for many months. I knew he was having a moral problem. I was probably the only one present who paid particular attention to his being there and one of the very few who knew he had a problem. As a body, we "happened" to be sharing Scripture with one another. To my amazement, one after another, people shared verses that had a direct bearing on this man's problem. Those who shared, of course, knew nothing of this man's moral problem. But the Holy Spirit did—and I was allowed to see God at work in a dramatic way through various members of Christ's body.

I firmly believe that this kind of experience should not be a rare one. Rather, our churches should be structured so that it can happen regularly. If we will only study the principles of Scripture and develop patterns that are biblically and culturally related, I believe God will do great things through His people. And this leads to our final step.

Step 3

Evaluate your church structures.

Many churches are not designed for "body function" but for "preacher function." Only the pastor or minister or some other teacher is delegated to share the Word of God with others in the church. Some pastors insist on being the only interpreter of Scripture. The Bible teaches that every Christian must be involved in this process. All Christians are to "speak the truth in love."

Don't misunderstand! It's very important for a pastor or teacher to open the Word of God through an extended exposition and message. I do this nearly every weekend. But it should not be the only means for communication. The Scriptures also place a strong emphasis on mutual and informal teaching.

Christians should meet together for the body of Christ to function—to encourage one another. This is why Paul wrote to the Colossians:

Let the word of Christ dwell in you richly as you teach and admonish one another with all wisdom (Col. 3:16).

What about your church? What are the patterns like? Is there freedom for every member of the body of Christ to function—"to encourage one another" and "to build one another up"? In large churches, small groups become the necessary means to allow this to happen.

DISCUSSION GUIDE FOR SMALL GROUPS

OPENING

Give each group member an opportunity to share briefly an experience in which someone encouraged them in a special way.

FOR DISCUSSION

1. Read Ephesians 4:14-16. Why is biblical truth the basic source for encouragement? In what specific situations have Christians encouraged you with biblical truth? In what situations have you been able to encourage others with the truth?

2. Read 1 Thessalonians 4:13–5:11. Why is encouragement and building one another up with scriptural truth lacking in our churches today? How can that be changed?

3. What does it mean to have "the word of Christ dwell in you richly" (Col. 3:16)?

4. Share experiences where someone has used words effectively—other than Scripture verses—to encourage you. Conversely, share some experiences where you have been discouraged and hurt. As a group, discuss how these negative experiences could have been handled differently.

5. Why is it important to also use the Word of God sensitively? How

can we "speak the truth in love" without making people feel we are using Scripture as a weapon—or even as a "club"?

CLOSING

Close your time together by celebrating the way you have built one another up in this group. Allow a time of informal affirmation, or choose one or more of the following options:

Invite each person to share a significant insight, a changed attitude, or a new way of living in relationship with others that has resulted from this study. Pray together, giving thanks for God's work in your lives.

Together look at the main topics of each chapter and list all the positive ways your small group has lived out these principles. Offer prayers of praise.

For Next Time

1. If you identified ways to apply the principles of this study that you would like to see implemented in your church, set a time to meet and discuss the best way to facilitate that implementation.

2. If your group wishes to continue studying together, consider using one of the other "One Another" books by Gene Getz: *Encouraging One Another* and *Loving One Another*. Both include discussion guides for small groups.

1. Gary Porter - Ankel
2. Adrey Legette
3. Tim Hart - Father
4. Baptist same sex marriage - Elaine sick
5. Election up coming election
10-21-12
6. Pam
7. Jackie Tue

8.

9. Norman Orns
10. Dave, Jenna

1-20-13
1. Leland Perry - Lungs -

2. Christ Smith

3. Cindy in bull da Leggette

4. Pam 2nd chem

5. Smyrers

6. 2-3-13

1. Church

2. Chris - In sea side

3. Pam - Her blood is low

4. B oarders

5. Jean Crandon]

6. Elaine Pike - Breathing

7. Ingrid - Going to Cal Feb 12 - March 12

8.